MOORE TO LYFE

By
TAMIKA FORD

Moore to Lyfe

Copyright © 2025 Moore to Lyfe. All rights reserved. No part of this publication may be reproduced, distributed, or transmitted in any form or by any means, including photocopying, recording, or other electronic or mechanical methods, without the prior written permission of the publisher, except in the case of brief quotations embodied in reviews and certain other non-commercial uses permitted by copyright law. Moore to Lyfe, its affiliates, assigns, and licensors retain all rights to this work. No claim to copyright is made for original U.S. Government works.

ISBN: 979-8-9925329-0-6

Foreword

Life doesn't always come with a roadmap. For me, the journey began with uncertainty, pain, and the constant struggle to find my place in a world that often felt unforgiving. *Moore to Lyfe* is not just my story! It reflects the challenges, lessons, and triumphs that have shaped who I am.

This book is for anyone who has felt alone, unheard, or trapped by their circumstances. It's for those who have dreams in their hearts but don't know where to start. Through my journey, I hope to show you that there's always a way forward, no matter where you begin. As you turn these pages, you'll witness moments of heartbreak, resilience, and the quiet strength it takes to rebuild from nothing. More importantly, you'll see the power of choosing yourself! Breaking free from expectations, healing from the past, and daring to imagine a better future.

Thank you for taking the time to walk with me through the chapters of my life. My hope is that you find pieces of your own story here and that it inspires you to live boldly, authentically, and without apology.

With sincere love and gratitude,
Tamika

Dedication

To my mom, whose love and lessons shaped the foundation of my strength. You are more than a mother; you are my angel sent from heaven.

To my brother, for always believing in me, even when I couldn't believe in myself. You brought the definition of living into my world.

To my sister, for always loving and appreciating me.
To my grandpa, whose wisdom and guidance will forever lead my steps.

To my husband, whose unwavering belief in me and constant encouragement inspire me to keep going, no matter life's obstacles.

To my children, for giving my life purpose and a reason to keep pushing forward every day.

To my cousin Cyn, for always being there and believing in my ability to touch and inspire millions. Your support has meant more than words can express.

To Shecosha, for standing by me and helping me when I needed it most.

And to everyone who believed in me, who gave me hope and motivation to share my story and help as many people as I can because the best is yet to come!

With all my heart, love, and gratitude,
Tamika

Prologue
A Moment

There was always someone to fear. You could feel it in the air, heavy and unspoken, like the walls themselves were holding their breath. The house carried a silence that wasn't peaceful, but watchfully waiting. Every step, every glance, every word had to be measured, because the wrong one could open a door you couldn't close.

We learned early how to move without sound, how to read the shifts in a room, and how to sense danger before it showed its face. It wasn't the kind of fear that screamed it whispered. It lived in the stillness, in the way shadows stretched too long at night, in the way the smallest noise could snap the air in half.

There are moments that brand themselves into you, moments you can never scrub away. A stare that lingers too long. A silence too heavy to carry. A presence that presses against your skin until you can't breathe. Those were the moments that taught us monsters don't always come from under the bed. Sometimes, they sit in plain sight.

And that was the truth we lived with, the monster was real. We just weren't supposed to say it out loud.

TABLE OF CONTENTS

Foreword iii
Dedication iv
Prologue: A Moment v
Introduction 1

Chapter One: I Am Who? 3
    Leave Behind the Usual 5
    Defying the Odds 7
    A Lot in Small Time 9
    Joy in the Bundles 10
    Everything Will Connect 12
    Simply Unforgettable Moments 13
    Time and Quantity 15
    Structure Behind the Front 16

Chapter Two: You Will Never Find Lost Time Again **19**
    Choices are Made from Change 21
    No pain medicine for a broken heart 23
    In front of your eyes are hard things to see 25
    Guidance Through Chaos 26
    Deception Runs Deep 28
    Power Over Innocence 29
    Truths Concealed Carefully 32
    Silent But Calculating 34

Chapter Three: Words Reflect Soul **39**
    Story behind the Walls 42
    Faith Over Fear 44
    Strength Through Struggle 45
    Love with Limits 47
    Heartache from love 50
    Shattered Trust 52

    Peace Beyond the Clouds... 53
    Hidden Battles Within 55
    Fighting Quiet Wars 60

Chapter Four: Consumptions of Weakness **63**
    Uncertainty Clouds Hope 65
    Broken, yet trying! 69
    Slither in the shadows 72
    Life flows within 74
    Ticking of the clock 76
    Dread of what's next... 78
    Strength feels Distant 79
    To Live is to Suffer...82
    Fear of Unknown 84

Chapter Five: Coming is a Change **87**
    Rain Before the Sun Shines.. 89
    Sprinkle of Hope..92
    The Words that Go Unheard 94
    Echos of Hurt... 98
    Beneath the Surface 103
    Mind Drifting Fear 106

Epilogue **111**

Acknowledgments **112**

About The Author.. **114**

Introduction

> *Life after a traumatic upbringing often feels like walking through the world with invisible weights, carrying burdens that others cannot see. The memories of pain, neglect, or fear can linger long into adulthood, shaping how we see ourselves and interact with the world. For many, a troubled past can seem like a prison limiting joy, connection, or personal growth. But deep within a quiet voice usually whispers there has to be Moore to Lyfe.*

Through inner strength, toughness, and reclaiming peace, people can discover purpose, joy, and fulfillment that transcend their earlier lives. Existence offers opportunities for new connections and self-discovery and allows individuals to build futures that are not solely defined by their childhood experiences. This belief that life can offer something splendid beyond the trauma is a powerful force.

This book explores that journey from the shadows of a dark livelihood to the light of self-discovery and resilience. It resonates with those who feel confined by their past and have wondered, "Is this all there is?" The last name, Moore, connects me to a specific family history, but it doesn't define the full scope of who I am or what my life can be. Like how there's Moore to Lyfe beyond your thoughts, there's also more to a person than a last name. The story doesn't end with the past or a name. It's just the beginning of hope, healing, and the promise of a future filled with purpose, connection, and peace.

My story, while not unlike many others in its moments of hardship and growth, is one that I feel compelled to share. It's not just about the things I've been through, but about the lessons I learned, the battles I fought, and the strength I discovered along the way. It's a journey from darkness to light, from a past that tried to define me to a future I'm still shaping. I hope anyone who reads this book feels inspired to keep going, never give up, and continue moving forward, no matter what challenges life may bring.

I want to tell my story, not because it's extraordinary, but because it's real. And maybe, just maybe, in telling mine, someone out there will feel seen, understood, or even inspired to tell their own. This is the raw, unfiltered truth of my life and pieces of my soul laid bare for the world to see.

This is my truth, and I'm ready to share it. There is more. This is my journey. This is my lyfe.

> *P.S. While this story reflects my journey through pain, resilience, and transformation, it also contains sensitive topics that may evoke strong emotions. I encourage readers to approach these pages with care and prioritize their well-being as they navigate them.*

Chapter One
I Am Who?

> *As a little girl, I always dreamed of being a princess. In my mind, everything would be perfect. I'd find the ideal husband, have beautiful children, and we'd be the picture of a loving, happy family. My life would be like a fairy tale, filled with joy, laughter, and everything I imagined happiness to be.*

As I grew older, I learned that life doesn't always follow the script we write in our childhood minds. The reality was far more complicated, with challenges I never could have predicted. Yet, through it all, I held on to that dream, believing that there had to be *Moore to Lyfe* than the struggles I faced.

All I wanted in life was to be loved unconditionally, as any normal person deserves to grow up in a nurturing home, protected and safe. In their purest and most innocent form, see the world through hopeful eyes, trusting that those around them will keep them safe. A child needs someone to depend on completely until they're old enough to stand alone on their own.

A child craves unwavering love without doubt, neglect, or selfishness. Love and affection are vital for a child's development, shaping who they become and how they see themselves. In those early stages, children learn about their worth and how to navigate the world around them. Without that foundation, the journey to adulthood becomes far more difficult.

Life can often feel like a battle, filled with challenges we never saw coming. We don't get to write our fate, and there's no manual to guide us through the ups and downs. As human beings, we are filled with countless questions like our purpose, pain, and the reasons behind our struggles but many go unanswered.

Instead of finding clarity, we sometimes bury our fears and uncertainties deep inside, sweeping them under the rug because confronting them feels too overwhelming. We avoid facing the hard truths head-on, hoping they'll fade, but life has a way of forcing us to reckon with what we've hidden. We might finally start to understand and grow in that reckoning.

Children, with their innocent minds, cannot fully grasp the complexity of it all, so we fill the gaps with questions:

- What do I do now?
- Can I stop him, or will I get hurt?
- Could he hurt me that badly?
- Can a kid really stop a grown-up?
- What would Mom think if she knew?
- Will I get in trouble if I do what he says?
- Is this my fault?

I was left with more questions than answers in this lifetime. Yet, somewhere deep down, I held on to the belief that one day, everything would make sense. For now, I was just a child that was innocent, wide-eyed, and wondering why the world suddenly felt so unfamiliar.

The echoes of laughter played in the background, children's voices chanting, "Eeny, Meeny, Miny, Moe! Tag! You're it!"

Who could have known that I was the one being chosen? Not for a game, but for a journey that would shape the rest of my life.

Leave Behind the Usual

It all began in a small city called Fort Wayne. My roots were deeply intertwined with this place's cornfields and quiet streets. Fort Wayne was known by some as a family-friendly city with the ideal for raising children at an affordable cost though many had never even heard of it. It was full of penny candy stores, family-owned restaurants, a mall, and local spots like the Boys and Girls Club. As a child, everything seemed so big: houses, cars, schools larger than life. For many, it was a quiet place to settle down, where even low-income families could make it. But for me, life started, and life took me where I never would have expected.

My mother, Dina, was a strong and determined young woman shaped by her upbringing. She was striking, with warm brown skin and long, flowing hair that danced in the wind. Joyful energy balanced her tomboyish charm, and her laugh was infectious. Yet, her eyes held a quiet, adventurous spirit. She had a glowing smile, smelled like fresh flowers, and dressed to perfection. Reserved but observant, she always seemed to see more than she let on.

Dina was not only a brilliant strategist but also had the heart of an angel. She navigated the world with sharp street smarts and an even sharper intellect. Her presence was magnetic; while she might blend in with her easygoing style, she stood out as extraordinary. Dina was one of the fastest-running track stars in school, effortlessly earning many medals. She graduated high school alongside her best friend, Cynthia, with dreams of a bright future.

In her late teens, my mom was in a casual relationship with a man who already had his own family. At first, it seemed innocent, a few shared laughs and moments of companionship, but things quickly turned when she discovered she was pregnant with me. With trembling hands and a heart full of uncertainty, she informed him of the news. His reaction was swift and cold because he didn't want any part. He explained that he did not want an outside child and returned to his family.

At that moment, my mother faced a choice that would define her life and mine. She could have easily succumbed to fear and doubt, but that was never her way. She wanted someone she could love and show a better life. She embraced the challenge head-on with fierce determination and decided to become a single mother. I often think back to that time and how brave she must have felt, yet how vulnerable she must have been.

As a young woman in a small city, she would have been met with judgment. But instead of letting that sway her, my mom leaned into her independence after graduating from high school and forging her own path. She found strength in her vulnerability, knowing she would bring me into a world where love would flourish despite the challenges. She took on jobs that didn't always pay well but allowed her to provide for us. She worked late nights and early mornings, sacrificing her dreams to ensure I had a fighting chance at life.

My mom, Dina, lived with her mother, Sharlean, and her stepfather, Majesty, while saving money even though their situation didn't look like the "traditional" family structure. Still, my mom's presence filled the house with love and abundance. She was the light in a home often surrounded by negativity. She made sure everything was ready for me before I arrived, even though she didn't get as much support from her own mother as she had hoped. She remained calm and still made a way out of no way.

At six months pregnant with me, my mother reconnected with Jefferson, someone she had gone to high school with. Jefferson was a man you couldn't forget. He stood tall with a slim build, his dark skin glowing under the light. His chiseled features, framed by neatly cut hair, exuded an understated handsomeness. His eyes were warm and thoughtful, often reflecting his quiet, introspective nature. He carried himself with a grace that turned heads. Though humble and soft-spoken, he was always generous with his time and kindness.

There was a quiet confidence about him that made him well-liked and admired. He was raised up to be a Jehovah's Witness, and his modest, conservative clothing reflected his religious beliefs. He wore collared shirts, dress slacks, or neatly pressed pants simple but clean. After graduation, they lost touch, but years later, they crossed paths again by chance, and something clicked.

What began as a simple reunion between old classmates quickly turned into something more, and soon they began dating. They rediscovered a connection that had been there all along. Despite the complexities of their living situations and being in two separate homes. My mom fell head over heels in love with him. To her, Jefferson was her knight in shining armor, sweeping her off her feet in a whirlwind of affection and promises. He showered her with love, making her believe everything would be okay, even in uncertainty.

Defying the Odds

On a frosty December evening in 1984, Dina, decided to indulge in a night at the movies to see *A Nightmare on Elm Street*, utterly completely unaware that her unborn child would make a dramatic entrance. I did somersaults in her belly during the film, eventually turning breech. When the time came for my arrival, I didn't just enter the world; I flipped my way into it. And here I am, a testament to the unpredictability of life from the very beginning.

In January, she gave birth to me at St. Joseph's Hospital. The doctors worked on me from the very start, their hands moving quickly to ensure I was okay. But even after I took my first breath, something wasn't quite right. I was just a newborn, too small to understand the world around me, but my tiny body was already battling a condition that made breathing difficult: bronchitis. Still delicate and growing, my lungs struggled to take in the air they needed. Each breath was a fight, each gasp a reminder that life doesn't always give you an easy start.

The doctors moved swiftly, their faces a mix of calm professionalism and urgency. Tubes and machines surrounded me as they worked to clear my airways, trying to get my fragile lungs to do what they were supposed to. My mother watched from a distance, her heart heavy with worry, powerless to do anything but hope that her little fighter would pull through.

It wasn't long before I was whisked away to the neonatal intensive care unit. I lay in a tiny incubator, wires attached to my chest, as the doctors and nurses monitored my every breath. They worked tirelessly, day and night, to ensure I had the strength to fight.

Despite all the chaos, a sense of quiet determination surrounded me. I may have been small, my lungs weak, but I was stubborn. I wanted to breathe, live, and grow. Slowly but surely, my body began to heal. The bronchitis loosened its grip on my lungs, and the doctors, who had been so worried at the start, began to see hope.

My mom handed the task of naming me over to her cousin, who decided on "Lamika" because she thought it would be fun for it to rhyme with her name, Rameka. That's how I got my name not from family tradition or a book of baby names, but from a spontaneous rhyme that connected me to my cousin in a way I didn't even know about. I entered the world dark-complexioned, with a head full of long hair, a tiny miracle ready to take on life.

Looking back, I realize that my struggle as a newborn set the tone for the rest of my life. From the very beginning, I fought to breathe. I fought to survive. I fought to prove that I could overcome whatever obstacles came my way. The doctors gave me a chance, but it was my own will to live that carried me through.

I am a testament to the unpredictability of life from the very beginning. And there I was, a little stronger because of it, knowing that even from day one, I was a fighter!

A Lot in Small Time

I can only imagine the joy and apprehension that filled their hearts at that moment. Jefferson embraced me as if I were his own child, with warmth and unconditional care. He came to visit us on a daily basis. My mom's heart swelled with joy and wonder at the sight of her firstborn, a love like no other blossoming instantly. She was embracing the reality of motherhood while still figuring out her own life.

Life with a newborn was a beautiful whirlwind of joy and challenges. Each day brought new experiences from the sleepless nights filled with gentle coos and cries to the heartwarming bonding moments during feedings. She marveled at every tiny milestone, from the first smile to the first grasp of their fingers. While exhaustion tugged at her eyelids, the overwhelming love she felt made it all worthwhile.

In mid-April, the weather was a blend of cool and mild temperatures, with frequent rain showers and occasional sunny days marking the transition to spring. Flowers bloomed, and trees regained their leaves. During this time, Mom began noticing she was feeling unusually fatigued. At first, she attributed it to the late nights spent caring for me. But as the days passed, she began experiencing strange cravings and an unsettling nausea that refused to subside. Pushing aside her concerns, she chalked it up to a stomach bug.

A few weeks later, She stood in front of the grannies bathroom mirror, holding a test that showed two pink lines, her heart racing. "This can't be happening," she thought. A sudden pregnancy was the last thing she had ever expected. They had always been careful, or so she thought. Mom was filled with a mix of excitement and fear. She remembered feeling a similar sense of uncertainty before. With a deep breath, she set up an appointment for an ultrasound to confirm.

The OBGYN confirmed, "Yes, you are pregnant." A thought that she'd already expected.

Mom urgently asked, "So, they'll be 11 months apart? Trying to process it all at once.

"That is correct, based on your last menstrual cycle and your ultrasound," the doctor replied.

Mom knew that Jefferson would be an amazing father, and she did not doubt that this child would be no different.

A few days passed, just enough time for mom to contemplate how to tell Jefferson the news. As she sat across from him, a mix of excitement and nerves churned in her stomach. After dinner, they sat on the couch, the warmth of the evening wrapping around them. Her heart raced as she searched for the right words.

"I've been meaning to tell you something," she began, her voice soft but trembling. He looked at her with a curious smile. She took a deep breath and gently placed his hand on her stomach.

"We're going to be parents again," she whispered, feeling both exhilarated and vulnerable. His face shifted through a range of emotions: surprise, wonder, and finally, a broad wide, glowing smile.

With her heart open and her fears slowly dissipating, she looked forward to the day she would hold their child in her arms. They sat silently in their own thoughts, letting the weight of those words settle between them as the reality of their new beginning sank in.

Joy in the Bundles

My mother got approved for a place and finally packed her things to leave, it was with a strange mix of relief and sadness. Dina loved her mom deeply, but she knew she needed space to find peace and stability for herself. Growing up at my grandmother's house was always a swirl of chaotic arguments, tension, and emotional rollercoasters. My mother felt like she was constantly walking on eggshells, never quite knowing what each day would bring. Dina reached out to her best friend, the Second Mother, Cynthia, to see if she wanted to share the place and go half on the bills with her. Cynthia agreed, knowing her best friend would find comfort in her support of being there.

Dina knew deep down that her best friend would love her children just as much as she did. Cynthia was like a sister to my mother. They would make a great team, sharing the responsibilities of bills and caring for the kids. Walking out the door that day, my mother felt the weight of years lift off her shoulders. It wasn't just about leaving home but choosing a healthier, quieter life. The children's father Jefferson would be able to come over freely now, and their family would be united in a new way.

On a cold winter night in December that same year, my baby sister was born. When Dina gave birth to her, it was like she brought a piece of sunlight into the world. My sister was born with a very light complexion and a head full of soft, long, dark hair. She was as beautiful as the sunset, delicate and glowing in her own way. Everyone who saw her couldn't help but admire her sweet little face and bright, curious eyes. She was perfect from the start.

Once again, my mom handed the naming over to her cousin, who loved rhyming names. She chose a name that matched mine and decided on Tareka. So, my sister and I both ended up with rhyming names, creating a kind of family rhythm that tied us all together in a playful, unique type of way.

The children's father was always there for Dina with love and grace. Together, they worked as a team to raise us to the best of their ability. Through every challenge, the parents stood by each other, showing us what it meant to be a family and filling our home with warmth, comfort and care. The Second Mother was also there to help, offering support and love whenever they needed it. With her assistance, our family felt even more complete.

Dina would clean the house while dancing to her favorite 1980s music blaring from the radio, her infectious energy filling every corner of the house. As she twirled and sang, we giggled in our cribs, captivated by her joy. Though Jefferson was working hard to provide for us and wasn't there during those lively moments, his love and dedication were always felt in the warmth of our home. My mother's smile was constant, lighting up her face as she watched over us with love and care. Dina took great pride in keeping our home spotless and dressing my sister and me like twins, with matching outfits down to our hair accessories.

Everything Will Connect

A little over a year passed in the blink of an eye, and when we were settling into life, Dina shared some surprising news that she was pregnant again, this time with a baby boy! The children's father Jefferson was thrilled about having a son. The news filled him with pride and excitement; he had always dreamed of having a son to share life lessons with and pass down his values. He envisioned teaching his son everything he knew: life skills, wisdom, and the lessons he'd picked up over the years. The anticipation lit up his face, and he couldn't hide his smile every time he spoke about the baby. For the man who loved her, this wasn't just about having a child; it was the beginning of a bond he had longed for his whole life.

My mother gave birth to Jefferson Jr. in February 1987, and suddenly, she had three little stair-stepper children: a two-year-old, a one-year-old, and a newborn. The new baby was a beautiful, dark-complexioned baby with smooth, chocolate-toned skin and short, fine hair that perfectly framed his little face. He was the very picture of sweetness and charm, with a smile that melted hearts and bright eyes full of wonder.

People often commented on how handsome he was, and the parents would beam with pride each time someone admired their handsome, chocolate baby. Because we were so close in age, the house was always bustling with little feet and baby giggles, and each of us reached new milestones one after the other. It was a lot for Dina and her partner to handle, but they took on the challenges with patience and love, embracing the beautiful, chaotic bliss of raising three stair-steppers all at once.

After Jefferson Jr. was born, my mom decided it was time to stop. As fertile as she was "you just had to breathe on her, and she'd be pregnant" she knew three kids were plenty. She decided to have her tubes tied, cut, and burned, ensuring that their little family would stay complete. It was a big decision, but she felt fulfilled with the three of us and was ready to focus all her energy on raising us the best way she knew how.

The children's father, however, was caught up in his faith and would have encouraged prayerful consideration of all medical decisions in line with Biblical principles. He had dreamed of having a bigger family, and the choice to stop at three children felt suddenly taken from him. When Dina went through with it, their relationship took an unexpected turn, creating a rift between them that wasn't there before. What had once been a shared journey of building a family together started to feel divided, with tensions neither of them had anticipated.

Though unmarried, the couple did their best to live the right way. Despite their efforts, challenges continued testing their strength and determination. They kept pushing forward and committed to creating a better life for us, even if the path wasn't always smooth.

Simply Unforgettable Moments

As the big sister to not one but two siblings, I felt an overwhelming surge of happiness and pride. Finally, I had real playmates which felt like a dream come true. No longer was I just the caretaker for my Cabbage Patch doll. That little doll had a unique face, a soft body, and a cute little outfit. It had been given to me on one of my birthdays, and it had been my only companion for a while. Playing with my Cabbage Patch doll and pretending to be a mom was a warm and nurturing experience. The memories of caring for something, even a doll, were incredibly meaningful. It was my little friend, and we shared a bond that filled my heart.

As my siblings arrived, that bond shifted. The joy of being their older sister was unmatched. I went from nurturing my doll to guiding my little siblings through the world, showing them the ropes and giving them all the love and excitement only a big sister could offer. Every moment spent together was a treasure, filled with laughter and unforgettable memories. We ventured into the world, facing adventures and challenges side by side, and I relished every second.

With the children's father by Dina's side, she had hoped for a promising future for us, but as the days turned into weeks and the weeks into months, the love she once felt for him began to shift. The sparkle in her eyes dimmed as she came to the painful realization that her partner was not the steadfast companion she had once imagined. The affection he had once showered upon her faded, replaced by a growing sense of uncertainty and doubt that seemed to hang over their relationship like a dark cloud.

We became matching triplets when our brother came along. It wasn't just about the close bond we shared as siblings; it was in the details. Our parents worked hard and rarely had to discipline us because we were obedient children. Their dedication to us was a beautiful thing to witness. We were always color-coordinated from the hair knockers to the socks and shoes. Our mother took great care in keeping our outfits well-maintained, and you would never catch her slipping when it came to how she dressed us.

We did everything alike, from the way we walked and talked to the way we dressed and styled our hair, all except for our brother of course. We even bathed together since we couldn't afford the extra water. It might have been easier for our working parents, but those moments turned into joyful splashes against the walls until the water ran out. In those times, we were in our happy place surrounded by each other, our mother and father, and our second mother living our best lives. Despite the unforeseen, those moments of togetherness, laughter, and love were our escape, our little world where we felt nothing but happiness and joy.

Time and Quantity

My parents took turns around their work schedules to ensure we had our bedtime stories, prayers, and goodnight tucks every night. Mom was a force of nature when it came to taking care of us, spending as much time as she could with us. She was a mother before anything else. We were her pride and joy, and every family function was a chance for us to shine, all dressed nicely and ready to enjoy another delicious home-cooked meal together.

Once, my sister and I thought it would be funny to pour flour all over our brother, take off his clothes, diaper, and put him on a pan in the oven while dinner was being made. We were just kids, full of mischief and curiosity. When Mom heard his cries, following the trail of flour to the kitchen, she set us straight quickly. I'm not sure if we were simply playing, but that moment reminds me of how kids mimic what they see, absorbing everything around them even if it leads to unexpected and sometimes chaotic moments.

Our daily routines were steeped in consistency, a pattern that shaped our childhoods. Mom would prep our hair, and we'd wear bonnets or even plastic Kroger bags to hold the styles in place. She laid out pressed clothes for us, packed lunches the night before, and each morning, she woke us up with a kiss, made breakfast, and saw us off to school. In the afternoons, she'd be there to greet us when we got off the bus, always ready with a snack and ensuring we were settled until dinner. After eating, we'd get our baths, be tucked in tight, and listen to bedtime stories. We recited the same two prayers every night.

Once we were asleep, Mom would head off to work, always ensuring she returned before we woke up. No matter how tired she was, she never left the house unpresentable—just a touch of lipstick, earrings, and her outfit pressed to perfection. Dad worked during the day, but he was home for dinner. And then there was Cynthia, who would pitch in to help whenever needed.

What Mom couldn't do, Cynthia gladly stepped in to care for us. She worked, too, but she always found time to bathe us, do our hair, and get us dressed. Cynthia was more than just Mom's best friend; she was indeed family. She loved us with the kind of care that only someone born to nurture could give. Sometimes I'd catch her and Mom playfully going back and forth about whose turn it was to take care of us. It almost felt like a little competition, but the kind filled with love.

Some nights, Cynthia would step in for Mom, giving her and Dad a break and allowing them to rest from their busy day. Cynthia would watch us when they worked, and she was like a second mom to us. She kept our hair neatly done, fed us, bathed us, and tucked us in with the same love and dedication as they had. And because she didn't have her children, she poured all that love into us. Working at McDonald's, she even brought us Happy Meals almost everyday, making us feel extra special. Cynthia loved making us smile, and it was impossible not to love her back.

Cynthia had a heart of pure gold. To her, we weren't just kids she cared for; we were her children in every sense of the word. Her love knew no bounds, and she embraced her role in our lives with open arms and an unshakable times. Cynthia was kind-hearted, caring, sincere, and always acted with purpose and good intentions. She was a loyal friend to Mom, a protector of our secrets, and an angel in our lives who walked this earth doing no wrong. She was trustworthy, dependable, and an all-around fantastic person; we all loved her dearly.

Structure Behind the Front

Mom and Dad worked as a team, balancing full-time jobs and taking us to appointments, outings, and the park. Jefferson was an amazing father! Mom was a multitasker and social butterfly, constantly checking in on others with a big smile. We went everywhere with her except work, and if she went out, Jefferson watched us. We adored our parents and saw them as perfect. Mom was my role model, setting high standards of care, positivity, and support for everyone she met.

Over time the laughter gradually vanished like a light snuffed out. Jefferson's breath carried a sharp, bitter smell of alcohol, and Mom's once-bright eyes grew hollow. The sparkle drained away slowly. The warmth that once filled our home was replaced by tense silence and sudden outbursts, and I felt lost, wondering if I was somehow to blame. Our happy family seemed to unravel before my eyes. Mom's radiant smile turned to tears, and our shared joy was replaced by shouting matches that left everyone feeling empty. My siblings and I were too young to grasp the reasons, but we felt its weight, which was heavy and undeniable. Dad clung to us, his love evident, yet it felt like we were all slipping into something dark and unfamiliar faster than any of us could stop.

Mom met a friend at work named Denny and invited him over while Dad was at work. When Jefferson walked in and saw another man in the house, panic set in. Denny bolted out the door, but Jefferson's fury was unstoppable. He attacked Mom, and in the midst of the violence, she was so terrified she had pooped herself. Crying and shaking, Mom called Granny, desperate for answers, unable to comprehend why Jefferson's rage had taken over.

Months have gone by in silence between the two. Mom sneaking seeing Denny, Jefferson drinking his problems away. Arguing started to become more normal than ever. Jefferson begged mom to stop doing what she was doing and oftentimes explained that he would die if he lost us from their disagreements. She felt as though their relationship had been shattered beyond repair. Eventually, Jefferson, broken and defeated, gave up on fighting for the family and moved out.

The love and laughter that once filled our home were now replaced with tension and pain. Mom lost in her pursuit of happiness and seemed willing to disregard the hurt she caused, no matter who it affected. It was as though something had a hold on her, strong enough to tear our family apart without a second thought. The emotions involved were undeniably overwhelming for me and my siblings to witness. It was heartbreaking! The loss of stability, safety, and the warmth of family was tough to process. We waited, convinced Dad would walk through the door as he always did. But that day, he never returned. Little did we know that what we were about to walk into would forever alter the course of our lives, an unspoken shift that would haunt us for years to come.

Chapter Two
You Will Never Find Lost Time Again

> *Dina moved on with her life as if nothing had happened, quickly adjusting to the new situation. It was almost as though the events that unfolded had no lasting effect on her. She began spending more and more time away from home, and being so young, we didn't know what the future may hold. We assumed she was at work, as usual. However, the once-warm and easygoing atmosphere in our home began to change. The dynamic between Dina and the Second Mother also started to change with time. They no longer spoke as much; when they did, it was a heated argument. They disagreed on nearly everything now, and the bond they had once shared seemed to unravel. The friendly, supportive energy that had always defined their relationship had vanished, leaving a void that no one knew how to fill.*

The children's father came over a few times, hoping to apologize again and work things out, but Dina gave him the cold shoulder, refusing to acknowledge his efforts. My mother faced a difficult decision: whether to try to work things out with Jefferson or move on with her life. This situation thrust her back into the world with a new relationship beginning to unfold. Cynthia, who was at work when everything happened, always supported Dina's choices, but deep down, she felt that Dina should have stayed with her first love. Though the Second Mother knew it wasn't her place to decide, she couldn't shake the feeling that Dina was making a mistake. Despite her doubts,

Cynthia continued to work and care for us, offering her support as best as possible.

Dina was happy again, and the sparkle in her eyes returned. For a brief moment, it felt like everything was back to normal. The Second Mother began to take on more of a motherly role independently ironing our clothes, doing our hair, and getting us off to school. One day, while visiting Granny, I noticed Dina had invited Denny over. She introduced us, saying, "These are my kids right here." Denny walked over and greeted us, saying, "Hi, my name is Denny. Nice to meet you guys." It was no time wasted; boom, we had a new man in our lives after the breakup.

We missed Jefferson more than we ever knew. Meanwhile, Dina started embracing our new life with Denny, creating a divide in our home. My mother told Cynthia that Denny would move in with her and the kids. It was a decision that left the air thick with tension. The Second Mother, although supportive, couldn't hide the concern in her eyes. She knew things were changing, and the comfort of their once-close friendship was slipping away. She didn't say much, but the unease lingered in the walls. Cynthia wore her heart on her sleeve, deep down holding in her true feelings and sparing Dina's.

Denny fit right in with us from the gate. He was a sincere, family-oriented man. About 5'9", slim, dark-skinned with a low-top haircut and waves, his eyes were often bloodshot red. I thought he looked strange, almost devil-like, but he seemed trustworthy and respectful. We spent time together as a family, with him helping Dina by keeping us in line, getting us ready for school, and doing fatherly duties around the house. Denny was put into rotation as if he had played this role prior. But little did we know something would happen that disrupted our lives, casting a shadow over everything we thought we understood.

A short time after Denny moved in, things began to feel weird. He wasn't acting like himself; something seemed off, as if his true nature was slowly revealing itself. You can sometimes catch someone watching you out of the corner of your eye? I started noticing the strange behavior: long, lingering stares, peeking around corners, the unnerving licking of his lips. I had never felt this way around the other men in our lives. His presence made my skin crawl, like bugs were crawling all over me.

As a little girl, I couldn't put my finger on the motive behind it all, but I knew something wasn't quite right. I tried to ignore it, running around the house, pretending nothing was wrong. But deep down, I felt a sense of fear I couldn't shake. This man was a stranger to me, and my instincts told me to stay wary, even if I didn't fully understand. Shortly after Denny moved in, things slowly began to spiral downward. A person can only keep up a façade for so long before their true colors show, and I noticed the changes in his behavior.

Choices are Made from Change

The Second Mother quickly noticed Denny's unsettling behavior and peculiar comments toward us. Like she was a fly on the wall, she kept a watchful eye on him in "mommy protective mode," making sure we were safe. She observed his every move, ready to intervene at any sign of trouble. Cynthia didn't trust him around us, and she made it her mission to keep us close, acting as our protector and willing to risk everything for our safety. Although she worked full-time, she adjusted her schedule to minimize the time we were left alone with Denny. Meanwhile, Dina, blinded by love and deception, couldn't imagine anything going wrong at home.

Denny was a master manipulator who used what he had to get what he wanted. He was highly observant and patient, carefully identifying those who seemed socially isolated or susceptible to influence. Denny excelled at building trust, often showering us with attention, compliments, and small gifts, making us feel unique and important.

In the initial stage of forming a friendship, Denny went out of his way to become someone we could lean on, positioning himself as a confidant, the "best friend" we never knew we needed. He was skilled at making us feel heard and understood, offering false security while subtly testing physical boundaries, perhaps with accidental touches, testing our reactions. He encouraged secrecy, asking us to keep our interactions private, creating a bond that isolated us and gave him greater control.

Once trust was established, Denny moved the relationship into deeper emotional territory. He began positioning himself as our protector, sometimes even as a boyfriend, further isolating us from friends and family. He manipulated our perception of what was normal, introducing sexual content or substances that lowered our inhibitions and cemented his hold over us. His behavior was erratic affectionate one moment, distant the next reinforcing our dependency on his approval. Throughout this stage, he continued to press for secrecy, convincing us that he was the only one who truly understood and cared for us.

The relationship eventually turned darker. His affection came with strings attached; it only showed up when we did what he wanted. If we didn't comply or show the level of obedience he expected, he would punish us. Little by little, his demands grew. He used words and emotions as weapons, breaking us down and convincing us that we owed him, whether it was loyalty, money, or something more he wanted. If we even thought about leaving, he made sure we feared the consequences. He would give us death threats against our lives and the lives of others we truly loved. His manipulation left us trapped and confused, like we were caught in a web we couldn't untangle.

Throughout this twisted plot, Denny capitalized on our emotional need for connection, gradually warping what should have been a parent-to-child relationship into something far more sinister. He maintained a façade of care and understanding while slowly destroying our sense of self-worth and autonomy. He wanted ultimate control over us and would stop at nothing to get it.

No pain medicine for a broken heart

The hurt in Cynthia's eyes was heartbreaking, and I could feel how much it took away from her. She loved us more than she loved herself, and would've laid down her life to protect us. The arguments escalated quickly, and in a cruel twist of words, Dina ordered Cynthia to move out immediately. The bond that had once been unbreakable was now shattered, and nothing would ever be the same again. The Second Mother moved out within a couple of weeks. She kissed us and told us how much she loved us. We cried, knowing we spent more time with her than Dina. Cynthia explained that she didn't want to leave but had no choice. We begged her to stay and asked her to talk to our mother about staying longer. The Second Mother just cried with us, comforting us as best she could.

Deep down, I knew she would worry about us every day she was away. She promised to visit as often as she was allowed. We watched sadly from the window as she packed her car and drove away. Denny was in the background watching the plot unfold. With our protector gone, he seemed almost gleeful. He started with small arguments with Dina, using them as an excuse to sleep on the couch. Sometimes, as we left for school, I'd catch sight of him peeking from above the covers. His eyes followed us, and just as Dina closed the door, I'd turn back to find his gaze lingering inappropriately. It was as if he resented the idea of us leaving for school, his expression dark and unsettling.

Denny was a master manipulator and pathological liar who could convince even himself of his fabrications. He would spin lies to keep us home from school while Dina was at work. "The kids were coughing all night. I think they should stay home today," he'd say with feigned concern. But Dina, ever practical, would reply, "I didn't hear any coughing, so they're going to school today." She knew staying home did us no good and clearly suspected nothing beyond his words. However, the thought of staying with him became increasingly uncomfortable for me.

Denny's mask was slipping. His charming façade crumbled, and his true intentions emerged with each passing day. The layers peeled back, revealing a man far from the doting figure he presented to be. He'd hold back less and less, with his demeanor turning dark as the night. The "nice guy" from before was now muttering cruelly under his breath, his presence looming large and menacing. I felt a growing sense of dread whenever he was near, his every move heavy with vindictive intent.

Dina being out of sight gave him more time to try different things. He barked orders with a rage that was impossible to forget, treating us like nothing more than nuisances. Any pretense of warmth was gone, and he now wielded his authority with cruel intentions on his prey. Behind closed doors, he became our tormentor, and we bore the brunt of his wrath. He very rarely left the house with "in and out" jobs. My siblings, too young to grasp the build-up over time, didn't sense what the future could possibly hold. We continued to fall back on what we knew, and that was each other.

He manipulated Dina expertly, planting seeds of lies that painted us as disobedient children. "Lamika told her siblings to shut up," he'd claim, or "Jefferson ignored me when I told him to go to the bathroom." Dina believed him, and we paid the price. No amount of obedience could shield us from the unjust punishments that followed. It felt like we were trapped in an unending cycle of helpless pawns in his twisted game.

Denny's sinister spirit had a hold on our souls. He needed to test how deeply Dina loved him and how far her trust extended into his fabrications. For him, it was a perverse game; for us, it was a nightmare we couldn't or wouldn't escape. He preyed upon the vulnerabilities of a fractured family, and I only wish Dina could have seen through his deceit in some type of way. If she would have just taken a second to look around.

In front of your eyes are hard things to see

Dina received a job offer down south, and with some family already living there, she saw it as a chance to start fresh, far from the pain and memories of our hometown. We packed up and moved to McComb, Mississippi, to a tall, white house that seemed grand but held its own set of strange challenges.

The porch, though charming, was infested with snakes. It became a place we avoided, and the fear of the creatures slithering beneath it kept us from stepping outside. My mother kept a broom by the door, always ready to swat away the snakes when we dared venture out. The heat in McComb was stifling, relentless, something we hadn't quite adjusted to yet.

We had a small, blue swimming pool in the front yard, a temporary escape from the Southern sun. Dina would fill it with water while she cooked in the kitchen, her gaze flicking to us through the window as she prepared hamburger meat mixed with pork and beans. Rek, ever the adventurous one, hopped into the pool without a second thought, only to immediately cut the bottom of her foot on something hidden beneath the water. It was just one more sign that things were never as easy as they seemed.

My sister was the life of the party, always outgoing, friendly, energetic, and always bringing joy to the room. When she cut her foot, though, she couldn't hide her frustration, and the tears started flowing. Dina rushed outside, quickly tending to her foot and telling her not to get back in the pool. Jefferson and I, more laid-back and easygoing, were content to keep playing in the water, oblivious to Rek's sadness. She sat on the ground, watching us, clearly upset that she couldn't join in.

Then, out of nowhere, Rek bolted across the yard, screaming and yelling at the top of her lungs. Dina rushed outside again, her face full of concern. It turned out that Rek had sat down in a pile of red ants, and they were biting her rear end. My mother didn't think twice; she scooped her up and rushed her to the bathroom, filling the tub with water and sprinkling something to get the ants off her. Those moments when Dina was home and spent time with us were the best. She was kind, always ready to help, and deeply cared for us. She was a people-pleaser, but above all, she did her best.

Denny, on the other hand, was a different kind of presence. He often paid attention from afar, watching us with a gaze that felt too intense and calculating. While Dina was nurturing, Denny had a knack for blending into the scene quietly, almost unnoticed, but always there, lurking just out of sight. His silence spoke volumes, as if he were biding his time.

Guidance Through Chaos

Dina signed me up for kindergarten at Otken Elementary in McComb, MS, and I immediately loved it. Meeting new friends felt exciting, and recess was the best part we could play and be free! School became my escape from the mishaps at home. I would have stayed at school all day if I could, not wanting to return to an eerie feeling. In the back of my mind, I couldn't leave my siblings, though. I was always worried about leaving them behind, but at such a young age, there wasn't much I could do.

One morning, Dina said, "Now, Lamika, make sure you smile for the camera. You've got picture day today!" She'd already laid out my outfit, perfectly ironed with crisp creases, and had done my hair in two high pigtails, each twisted down with a barrette at the end, just touching my shoulders. I felt cute, and for a brief moment, everything felt normal.

I remember lining up for kindergarten pictures, and back then, we took two class photos, one at the beginning of the year and another at the end. We all had to walk in a single-file line onto a three-tier bleacher in the gym. The photographer would say, "Okay, teachers, get in on both ends, and on the count of three, smile!" Then she would count, "1, 2, 3… FLASH!" As soon as she said "3," my eyes were squinted shut. I hated the flash from the camera; it hurt my eyes. I was more scared of the flash after the picture was taken. Unfortunately, I knew my eyes were glued shut. Hopefully Dina would see that I smiled for the camera though.

We had to stay in place for a few seconds after the photo was taken. I remember thinking my eyes were wide open, looking directly at the camera lady, but when the picture came back, I was the only one with my eyes closed. Once the pictures were developed, Dina was super upset when she saw it. I really wanted that picture-perfect moment. That moment made me realize something important: I knew I was different from everyone else in the photograph.

Even at such a young age, I knew I was meant to be a helper, a leader, and a motivator. I found myself trying to guide people in the right direction and treating everyone equally, no matter what. Deep down, I dreamed of becoming a nurse, someone who could bring healing and comfort. I would picture my older self helping people with their medicine, assisting them in their daily living, and seeing their faces light up with relief because they felt cared for. That vision became my safe place, my happy place, and the spark that kept me moving forward.

We had grown accustomed to our new life in the Mississippi culture of talking, walking, and eating like everyone around us. My siblings and I had even picked up saying "ma'am" and "sir" after every word, fully embracing the Southern environment. For about a year, things seemed to flow smoothly. But eventually, we moved back to Fort Wayne. Life in Mississippi had started to wear on Dina, being far away from her family, trying to balance work and home, and not having the support she truly needed. She couldn't do everything alone, and Denny wasn't much help. The weight of it all was too much for her to carry by herself, so going back home felt like her only option.

Leaving wasn't easy for me, especially since I had grown attached to the friends I made there and the life we had built. Still, there was a sense of relief knowing we would be closer to family again. Dina believed going back was the best decision for us, even though things hadn't worked out the way she imagined down south. As we packed our bags, we carried both sadness and hope. The sadness for what we were leaving behind, and hope that a new start back home might give us the stability we needed.

Deception Runs Deep

But even as we returned home, Denny was still on his path of destruction, leaving us unsure of what battles we would face next. Every day, it was something new. He always knew exactly what to say to twist the truth and get what he wanted. He would say to Dina, "I've been wanting to tell you that Tareka has been looking at me a lot," or "Lamika comes and sits on my lap all the time." These were the little seeds planted to build his narrative. He knew how to manipulate the situation, using any opportunity to turn Dina against her own children.

Dina believed half of what he told her. Deep down, I think she felt something in her heart wasn't right. But Denny always twisted it, making it seem like we were the ones initiating these different scenarios, and he had a way of turning every situation to his advantage. Little by little, I began to see through him. He wasn't just stirring up trouble; he was moving toward something bigger, something built on lies and deception.

This particular day, Dina came into our room to read us a bedtime story. As usual, we pleaded with her to stay home, hoping she would. She gently explained that the bills needed to be paid so we'd have a roof over our heads. After our prayers, she kissed us and said, "Love y'all." We watched her hurry downstairs, grab her winter coat, and disappear around the corner as she headed for work. She left us with a monster hiding in the shadows.

As soon as the door clicked shut, he crept to the window and peered through the blinds, watching intently as her car disappeared down the street. This was his time to execute his plan. Without a word, he slipped into their bedroom, grabbed a blanket, and quietly descended the stairs. He settled onto the couch, his movements nervous but eerie. Then, out of nowhere, his voice boomed through the house, "Lamika, COME DOWN HERE!" The sound of his voice sent chills through the floor; we all began silently crying, instinctively knowing that when an adult called our names like that, it usually meant someone's in big trouble.

Tareka and Jefferson whispered in a frantic tone, "Mik, please don't go down there. Stay here with us." I looked at them in fear for my life, torn between anxiety and uncertainty. There were so many thoughts swirling in my head. Minutes passed, and I still hadn't moved off the bed. I decided to stay upstairs, clinging to the hope that if I stayed still, the moment might pass. I felt in my heart something wasn't right. I comforted my siblings the best way I could, pulling them close, wrapping my arms around them, and whispering, "It's going to be okay," even though I wasn't sure myself. I was thinking, I could possibly go downstairs, and they would never see me again.

Then his voice broke through the silence, louder and sharper this time. "If you don't come down here, you're getting a whooping," he yelled. My heart pounded as tears streamed down my face. I was crying hysterically now, my small body trembling with fear. Finally, I slid out of bed, my little feet hitting the cold floor. I turned to Tareka and Jefferson, my siblings, and whispered through sobs, "I'll be back."

Power Over Innocence

As I moved toward the stairs, my mind raced. At that exact moment, my limbs were shaking to the core. I told myself I had to be tough, though I didn't understand why. I couldn't understand what business a grown man had with a child who should've been asleep, resting for school the next day. Dina had already tucked us in for the night, and that's where we were supposed to stay. Safe in our beds, not being called out for reasons that didn't make sense. The fear of the unknown loomed large, but so did the weight of survival. I stepped forward, unsure of what awaited me but knowing I had no choice.

Every step I took felt like I was descending into a dark abyss, as if each movement pulled me further from safety and closer to an unimaginable fate. The sensation gripped my tiny mind, filling it with a profound dread that made it hard to breathe. It was an indescribable moment in time. I took forever to get down that flight of stairs. I focused on each step, watching my feet: right foot step, left foot step, and repeating it in my head.

My nerves were so bad my whole body was shaking as I walked, every step unsteady like my legs could barely hold me up. I got a third of the way down and peeped around the opening into the front room. He was sitting there, looking at me. My heart was pounding so hard it felt like it had detached from its vessels, beating outside my body. I continued down the stairs, each movement felt weighted down, as if twenty-pound weights were strapped to my legs holding me back. When I reached the bottom, I walked over to him. He said in a rage, "Come closer to me."

"WAIT!" I said. "Why are you grabbing me like that? What did I do? Am I in trouble?" The skin on my arm balled up in his hand. My arm started going numb from resisting his grip. His voice filled with anger. "Get over here! OR ELSE! I will make certain your siblings won't see the light of day." The white around his eyes turned red. I continued to pull my body weight in the opposite direction. His voice carried over to the next apartment as he called my siblings to come downstairs. At that very moment, I had a choice to make: Either I give in or suffer the consequences. I said sadly, "Alright! Ok, I'll stop. Please, leave them alone." His voice changed as he yelled, "Don't move from that bed unless I call y'all down."

At that instant, I gave up fighting for anything I believed in. My heart thumped in my chest, a steady reminder that I was no longer resisting. He said, "GET UNDER HERE!" I could feel the itchy, rough, prickly wool fibers on my skin. The throbbing and sharp pain shooting through my body was unbearable. My brain felt like a ball being bounced around in my skull. "OUCH…OHHHHH….STOP IT." My muscles screamed as if they were being torn apart.

Each breath sent daggers stabbing through my chest. My body felt like it could not breathe; all I could do was take a deep breath, filling my lungs with air, and holding it in. "LET ME GO," I mumbled breathlessly! I was gasping, lungs clawing for oxygen, but never catching up. The tingling sensation on my cheek from his palm made me go silent. I started to notice tiny white dots on his nose from a growling face he made. With his breath on my neck, he lets out a "GRRRRRRRRRRRR!" sound. He shoves my body to the side. Out of breath, he let out a long 'Ahhhhh,' before saying, "Now go upstairs and lie down."

I felt an outrageous sense of anger. The walls I had built around myself crumbled, exposing me to the raw, uncertain reality of what I had encountered. My mind raced at a thousand miles a minute, overwhelmed by feelings of betrayal, hurt, shame, uselessness, and misuse. Time seemed to freeze, leaving me trapped in a whirlpool of uncertainty, questioning what control I really had over my life. His voice was cold and sharp, slicing through the silence as he ordered me to pull myself together and tell my sister to come down, and a chill ran down my spine at the command. I summoned every ounce of strength I had left, my body trembling as I limped up the stairs, determined to follow his command even though each step felt like a battle against my own fear.

My siblings waited for me, their shirts soaked with worried tears, their eyes pleading for reassurance. My spirit screamed for me to tell them to run, but fear clung to my face like a mask as I sent my sister away, forcing her to face what I had just endured. My words lay frozen, choked in my throat, unable to break free as I braced for what was to come. Tareka said, "No, I don't want to, don't make me go," "Mik," her voice trembling with fear. I had to coax her, my heart breaking as I told her we wouldn't make it through the night if she didn't go.

I summoned the strength of a lion, knowing that if I faltered, we would all crumble. I dragged myself up to the bed, pulling the very marrow from my bones as if extracting the last remnants of my strength, each movement an agonizing testament to the battle within me. Lying there, stiff as a board with tears streaming down my face like a river, I whispered, "I want mommy," and at that moment, a tiny arm wrapped around me. Jefferson couldn't understand the full extent of what happened, he just knew we were sad. We shared the pain quietly, finding small comfort in each other's embrace.

I woke up feeling water on my skin, the sweet soap filling my nose as a hand moved back and forth, scrubbing us from head to toe. The dim light barely cut through the heavy darkness, casting long shadows that seemed to stretch on forever. We were instructed to get dressed quickly and return to bed, the weight of the night pressing down on us like an unspoken promise. Huddled together, my siblings and I wrapped ourselves in blankets, the chill of the room seeping into our skin. Denny stood over us and said, "If anyone speaks on what happened, I will kill you all one by one. Don't EVER tell a soul, not even your mom. She won't believe you all anyways." He hurried up, showered, and laid in bed awaiting Mom's return. We clung to each other, silent tears streaming down our faces as we cried, seeking comfort from one another. Sleep came slowly, a fragile refuge that offered no answers but a momentary escape from the unrelenting night.

Truths Concealed Carefully

I always imagined that parents could read the minds of their children, and since Mom had me, I thought I was part of her, so she should know exactly what I was thinking or feeling. My siblings and I scurried to the kitchen to greet Mom. Jefferson charged for the stairs first yelling, "Mom is here." I was praying Jefferson didn't say anything about the night before as we are hugging Mom's leg. Denny walked into the kitchen and kissed her on the cheek. He said, "Hello, beautiful! I got you feeling extra amazing this morning, huh?" Mom just laughed with joy as she continued cooking breakfast. As his tall frame walked past us he immediately looked down at our faces, daring us to say a word. Interrogating us with his half smile and treacherous grin. The silence was thick and unspoken as if speaking would break the fragile thread holding us together. Denny continued with his normal routine, a relentless, unbothered, steady drumbeat soul.

I wanted to tell my mom so bad what happened, but the urge just wouldn't let my words form in my mouth. Could she be disappointed? Would she trust me anymore? I should be able to talk to her about anything, but Denny ensured we didn't speak. The silence between us grew, and the weight felt like a wall I couldn't break down. I longed to confide in her, to explain everything, but the fear of her reaction and his intimidating stares would leave me trapped in quiet turmoil.

It was as though the world had fallen into a strange, unfeeling place where time stretched on endlessly, turning days into weeks. As the first light pushed through the blinds every morning, he would wait patiently until Mom left for work, then call my sister and me down the stairs. The air would crackle with a tension we couldn't name, and we'd go, heart pounding, minds racing to brace for what was coming next.

This particular day, I was heading down the stairs, each step pulling me closer to what I already feared. The creaking wood beneath my feet seemed to whisper secrets, and the air was thick, suffocating. Just as I reached the last step, a sudden awareness prickled at my senses. I turned slightly to see a glimpse of Jefferson right behind me, his presence so quiet I hadn't noticed it until now. His eyes met mine, wide and shadowed, the tension between us thickening with every heartbeat.

My body froze, heart pounding, rooted to the spot, while tears streamed down my face, hot and relentless, and snot trickled down my cheeks, leaving trails I didn't care to wipe away. "Leave my sisters alone!" Jefferson yelled. I felt something was wrong when he bit his leg, the sound sharp and sickening. Denny's voice roared through the apartment, shaking the walls and cracking the silence, and his eyes were wide with disbelief, searching for answers that didn't come.

"Jefferson, stop!" I screamed, but my voice was thin, tremulous, a whisper swallowed by the chaos. Jefferson's small fists pounded at Denny's leg, each strike filled with fury and desperation. His voice was a mixture of defiance and fear as he screamed, "Stop messing with my sisters!" He roared, "LEAVE THEM ALONE." Our little protector didn't even have a clue but to defend the ones he loves. Jefferson put all his strength and might into helping us as much as he could.

But Denny didn't flinch. His eyes narrowed, and in one fluid motion, he swept Jefferson up by one arm, slung him high in the air and slammed him down onto the top of the refrigerator. The metal crunched beneath Jefferson's weight, the sound broke the stillness that hung in the room. Denny stood back, arms crossed, eyes fixed on Jefferson as if he were a trophy of control. He left him there, still and full of rage, hours stretching long after he'd turned his attention away, turning to my sister and me with a smile that cut deeper than any words could.

"Now," Denny said, his voice a low growl that cut through the tension like a blade, "and I dare you to jump off. GO AHEAD, JUMP, jump down, and save your sisters." A chilling laugh spilled from him, echoing 'Ha… ha… ha…' like something out of a nightmare." Jefferson, filled with a fire no one could put out, balled his fist up and silently growled with fury.

Silent But Calculating

The kitchen seemed to shrink, the space between the sofa and the refrigerator now a chasm too wide to cross. The room pulsed with a heavy silence as Jefferson stared at me, eyes furiously glistening, a mixture of confusion and anguish. I couldn't move; I couldn't breathe. I was trapped in a moment where my world spun on a different axis. The fear curled into something sharp and curious as I glanced up and saw my brother perched on top of the refrigerator, eyes panicked, searching for escape.

"Tareka, go back upstairs until you're called down." Denny's harsh voice sliced through the heavy air like a whip, leaving a sting that lingered long after the words were spoken.

Tareka flinched, her small body shuddering as she looked at me, her eyes round and shimmering with unshed tears scared to be upstairs alone in addition to checking on Jefferson all at once. I couldn't speak or move as she hesitated, searching my face for a signal that might tell her it was okay to stay.

But I couldn't give her that. The silence between us was a shield, a barrier too thick to break. Without a word, she turned and ran up the stairs, the creak of each step a testament to her fear, the sound swallowed by the cold quiet of the room. Tareka's footsteps faded, and with them, the last echo of innocence. I could still feel her presence in the room, a specter of the life we once had, a life that Denny's presence had erased piece by piece. And now, it was just me, Jefferson, and that look in Denny's eyes that I knew would haunt us the rest of our lives.

"No! Let me go! Oh, stop! Please, don't!" The pleading slipped out of me, a broken prayer, but it was too late. I wanted to fight, scream for help, and tell anyone who would listen what was going on. I tried to run, tear myself away from the suffocating reality, and disappear into that happy place where I was safe. My gown pulled up to my neck and all the moans made me sick to my stomach. Mentality was unreachable! My heart throbbing out of my chest as I forced myself to look away from Jefferson, who sat frozen in the moment, eyes fixated on me, his small body trembling in the shadow of a promise he couldn't keep.

I closed my eyes as my body went numb and let my mind drift to my happy place. It was full of colors, drawings, and sunshine. In this world no one could hurt me. I ran through tall grass with my arms stretched wide, eating fruit straight from the trees. The grapes were as big as apples, and candy grew on branches like leaves. I convinced myself this was heaven. I had to believe there was happiness somewhere.

In my mind, it was me and my siblings running free, chasing each other, laughing with joy. There was no sadness here.

Back in the room, he let out a low, frustrated growl "Grrrrrrr" of disappointment with me as my body lay limp, offering no reaction. "Oh, so it didn't hurt? Just wait 'til next time," he snapped, still breathless. In that moment I knew he wanted me to fight, to resist, to beg him to let me go. But the pain was so unbearable my body had already shut itself down.

Jefferson's eyes remained stuck on the scene, dark pools filled with confusion and anguish. The innocent light that used to dance in us was now dimmed, swallowed by the terror of that day. He had always been the fearless one, the protector in his own way, and in this moment he was too small to help me, too vulnerable to save himself. Once he composed himself, his eyes locked on Jefferson with the cold satisfaction of someone who had claimed a trophy of power. He called me back down just as Denny turned, the room shifting with his movement. His eyes met mine, icy and unforgiving, like shards of broken glass. "Now, do you understand?" His voice was low and measured, a warning laced with something more sinister.

I swallowed, the lump in my throat heavy and burning. I nodded, eyes stinging with unshed tears. It wasn't just fear for me; it was fear for Jefferson, Tareka, and the part of us that was still whole and would never be again. He leaned against the counter, arms crossed, his expression unreadable. "Good. Now, let's get this straight. No more interruptions, no more games. You got that?"

I nodded again, a whisper of a promise escaping me. But the air felt thick with lies, the kind you tell yourself to survive.

Finally, after a few hours, he let Jefferson down, the tension releasing with a suffocating finality. "Don't ever do it again, or I'll kill you," he spat, the threat ringing in the space between us like a cruel lullaby. That night, we didn't talk. We didn't dare. And when the world finally grew quiet, and Denny left the room, I looked at Jefferson. The shadow of what he had witnessed hung over him, over us all, but there was something else in his eyes, too something more profound. It was a flicker of resolve, a silent vow that one day, things would change. It was the beginning of something that couldn't be snuffed out, even in the darkest of times.

Chapter Three
Words Reflect Soul

> *Despite it all, I knew then that even in the darkest moments, there was a light that couldn't be extinguished, not by the cruelty of the night or the monsters that lurked in it.*

When it got too hard to breathe, I'd close my eyes and go to my special place, a world only I could see. There was a little pond that shimmered like diamonds, frogs that wore crowns made of flowers, and laughter floating through the air like music. The wind whispered my name gently, telling me I was still loved, still whole, still here. I'd spin in circles until I fell into the grass, staring up at clouds that shaped themselves into hearts and wings. In that world, I was free. In that world, nothing hurts.

From that day on, Jefferson never intervened again. The fire in his eyes dimmed, replaced by a shadow that haunted him, and the silence that followed was louder than any noise. It was the silence of fear, of secrets that couldn't be shared, of a bond that Denny was determined to shatter.

Mom pulled out all the stops for my 6th birthday, making it feel like the biggest event of the year. The yard buzzed with laughter and the smell of sizzling food, and the energy was electric. She spent time doing my hair, the bright knockers clicking as she twisted my long pigtails. When she was done, I looked in the mirror and saw a perfect little Barbie doll staring back.

Then, she introduced someone new, a man standing just on the crowd's edge. "This is your cousin, Kinney; he goes by Kin," she said, her voice almost too bright. He stepped forward with a big grin that didn't quite reach his eyes. "You look so pretty on your birthday," he said, his tone sweet but unsettling.

I twirled in my dress, letting the skirt flare out, and said, "Thank you!" His gaze lingered a second too long before he stepped back into the crowd.

Family members kept arriving with colorful bags and boxes, shaking the cold off their coats as they stepped inside. The air smelled like fried chicken, pound cake, and cocoa butter. Aunties laughed loud from the kitchen, unwrapping foil pans, while uncles crowded around the table arguing about the game. Boots lined the hallway, and the heat from the furnace mixed with the sound of R & B music playing low in the background.

We played hide-and-seek between coats and gift bags, shrieking and giggling while the grown-ups yelled, "Y'all better not mess up this house!" When everyone finally circled to sing "Happy Birthday," my heart raced as Mom carried out the cake. The candles flickered from the warmth of our laughter and the hum of love that filled the room.

I loved the cake, especially how it always had my name, age, and "Happy Birthday" written in big, bold letters. As I made a wish and blew out the candles, I wished to be free from hurt, harm, and danger. I wished that me, Mom, and my siblings could live happily ever after. At that moment, I felt like the happiest girl in the world, completely unaware of how quickly things could change.

After the party, Kin stayed the night, he started staying multiple nights almost like he lived with us. At first, it seemed harmless. Mom had a big heart and trusted people too quickly, always calling them "family." We met a new family member after each gathering. But something about Kin felt...didn't feel right.

Sometimes, Mom and Denny would get into heated arguments and the walls seemed to vibrate with their anger. Denny would storm out the door, and Mom, always working hard to keep a roof over our heads, would leave Kin in charge of us. "He's just staying for a little while," she'd say, her voice weary but sure, as if saying it made it true.

Kin wasn't like anyone we'd been around before. He acted more like a woman than a man, his movements too flamboyant, his voice too soft. He was tall, with light skin and good hair, features everyone commented on, but his frame was thin, almost frail. His breath always carried the sharp sting of alcohol, and there was a creepiness about him that made my skin crawl.

At first, it was subtle: the way he played in my hair and the squeezing of my shoulders too long and how he always found reasons to grab on to us. Then it escalated. He'd find ways to get me or my sister alone, his hands too familiar, too invasive. He'd whisper things we didn't understand but knew weren't right, his fingers venturing where they had no business being.

I remember freezing, the air leaving my lungs, and my body trapped in a haze of confusion and fear. My sister and I didn't talk about it. Maybe we were scared, or perhaps we thought no one would believe us. We never thought about telling anyone, out of fear of the unknown, fear of what would happen if we did. So we carried it in silence, pretending everything was normal, even when nothing felt that way inside.

Had we become easy targets? Did we carry some invisible mark that drew predators like moths to a flame? I wondered if something about us screamed "vulnerable," as though being hurt before made us easier to hurt again. The thought gnawed at me, a constant ache in the pit of my stomach as if we were walking around with a broken shield, too worn to protect us. It was as if the weight of our past pain had etched itself into our very being, making us stand out to those who thrived on causing hurt. Each encounter and glance felt like another reminder that our vulnerability wasn't just a part of us, it was all we seemed to be to the world.

Kin eventually found a place to live and moved out, but even then, it didn't feel like he was really gone. His presence stayed with us quiet, heavy, and hard to forget. A constant reminder that once again, we weren't safe in our own home. The moments piled up like a weight on my chest, a burden I didn't know how to carry or escape. And still, the world around us carried on, oblivious to the storm raging in our small, fragile lives. His absence didn't erase the scars, but it did offer a glimpse of relief as if the air around us had finally started to clear. Yet, the shadows of his presence lingered, haunting the spaces where we once tried to find peace.

Story behind the Walls

Some do not always understand why people come back around. You just know how they make you feel. The feelings of being nervous, sometimes trapped, sometimes wishing you could disappear. Denny showed up again like nothing bad had ever happened. Everyone acted normal, so I tried to do the same. But inside, something felt off like my stomach dropped every time he walked in the room. It was like something about him made the house feel smaller, like there wasn't enough space to feel safe.

One day, his voice echoed through the house, calling for me and my sister. Something in his calm but commanding tone made my stomach churn. I hesitated at the bathroom door; the steamy air was thick and suffocating as it mixed with the chill of dread coursing through me. Denny stood inside the shower, completely unclothed, water streaming down his twisted expression. He gestured for us to come closer, his eyes dark and empty of anything human. Tareka sat quietly on the toilet, her small hands gripping the seat's edge as if trying to anchor herself from floating away in fear.

"I want you to come here," he said, his voice low but edged with a threat I didn't dare test. My body was stiff, and my feet felt cemented to the tiled floor. I shook my head slightly, hoping he'd change his mind, but instead, he pointed to me, then to the shower. He yelled, "NOW."

I stepped closer, my movements mechanical and detached, as if my mind were trying to protect me by pulling me somewhere far away. His next words were cruel and deliberate. "Take your clothes off and get in."

My hands shook as I pulled my dress over my head, every fiber of my being screaming at me to run, but I couldn't. I couldn't leave Tareka. She needed me. I glanced at her, our eyes locking for a brief moment. She looked so small, her gaze heavy with confusion and shame she couldn't yet put into words.

Stepping into the shower, the scalding water stung my skin, but the pain was nothing compared to what came next. He grabbed my hand, his grip rough and unforgiving, and pressed it to his private area. My stomach churned, and my mind spun in circles, desperate for an escape.

"Move it," he ordered, his voice cold and emotionless. I froze. His grip tightened, and he hissed, "Move your hand back and forth."

Tears blurred my vision as I obeyed, the humiliation burning through me like wildfire. "FASTER," he demanded. When I hesitated, his hand struck hard across my face. My cheek went numb as the world spun. I slipped, hitting the shower floor, my palms slapping against the wet tile. For a moment, everything went quiet except for the sound of rushing water. I touched my face and pulled my hand back with red smeared across my fingertips. My heart pounded so loud it drowned out his voice. I wanted to disappear, to sink straight into the drain and never come back.

I just laid there, water beating down on me, the sound of it mingling with my sister's soft sobs from the toilet. My heart broke not for myself, but for her. She was watching this, learning from it, and I couldn't protect her. Denny loomed over me, a dark shadow with no trace of remorse. At that moment, I realized he was not only trying to hurt me, but erase every piece of safety and innocence I had left. And worst of all, I didn't know how to stop him.

Once he finished with me, Denny ordered me out and called my sister in. I sat on the toilet, trembling, forced to hear what I couldn't stop. Afterward, he made us wash ourselves as if water could cleanse the filth of what he'd done, then sent us to bed like nothing took place.

Faith Over Fear

Jefferson was left to his own world, oblivious or pretending not to know. But with my brother... I dreaded the thought of him suspecting anything. The shame clung to me, with every breath, leaving me hollow as a child, broken and discarded like something used and unwanted. It was best to stay focused and devise a plan to get us out of this nightmare.

Months passed in a blur, and then, Tareka did the unthinkable. Every night, Mom dressed us in long, white silk nightgowns with matching white panties before sending us to bed. It had become a ritual, a chilling one. That evening, Mom had just come home from work, her presence a weary comfort. As she sat on the edge of the toilet, the bathroom door creaked open, and my sister, still restless, snuck out of bed. She missed Mom so much she waited for her to get off. She snuck right into the bathroom.

Mom's voice was softer than usual, almost casual, as she spoke. My sister sat cross-legged on the floor, her wide eyes taking in Mom's rare moment of stillness. But then, in the dim light, a sharp, crimson stain caught Mom's attention. "What is that?" Mom's sharp and probing voice cut through the silence. Tareka's gaze dropped. Her small body trembled, and silent tears trailed down her cheeks. The room seemed to hold its breath.

"HAS DENNY BEEN…?" Mom's question hung in the air, a whispered accusation that shook the walls. The smoke from her Virginia Slim curled in lazy waves, mingling with the heavy tension. She started to sway, eyes glistening with fury and something else—an unspoken gut-wrenching disguise.

"Tareka, PLEASE TALK TO ME. TELL ME, BABY, HAS HE…?" Mom's voice cracked, trembling as she reached for the truth. Tareka's eyes locked with Mom's, dark pools brimming with unspeakable pain. "Ye, Denny…" she whispered, barely audible, but it pierced through the heavy silence. The room seemed to freeze, each second stretching into an eternity.

Mom's face contorted with rage, her voice a raw, guttural scream. "I'm going to kill him. I'm going to destroy him. I can't believe this! WHY, LORD? Why my babies? They are innocent; they've done nothing to no one! How could he do this?"

The fury that erupted from her was almost tangible. Her steps were heavy as she stormed out of the bathroom, eyes locked on the ironing board. Without hesitation, she ripped the iron from its place, yanking the cord out of the socket with a swift, violent motion.

Strength Through Struggle

Denny lay in the bed, tangled in restless sleep, oblivious to what was coming. Mom's shout sliced through the night, shaking the house, and he jolted awake, eyes wide with shock. It was as if he had seen a ghost, paralyzed by the realization.

"YOU DID THIS TO MY BABIES!" Mom's voice roared, each word fueling the fire blazing inside her. Before Denny could speak, before he could defend himself, Mom swung the iron, the cold metal connecting with a sickening thud.

A silence fell, heavy and suffocating. Denny's body crumpled, lifeless, and limp, the room echoing with a stunned, breathless quiet.

We held our collective breath. The line between relief and terror blurred in the night.

Denny lay unconscious on the floor, a dark pool of blood spreading beneath him, seeping into the cracked tiles. Mom stood over him, her eyes wide, reflecting a mix of shock and disbelief. The iron, now dark with his blood, slipped from her fingers, falling to the ground.

Without hesitation, she rushed around the house, her breathing erratic and her eyes wild as she gathered our belongings. We huddled together in the corner by the front door, eyes moving nervously between Mom's frantic movements and the dark empty space behind us. She zipped our bags with sharp, decisive motions, the weight of her actions pressing down on the room.

In moments, we were in the car, the air thick with tension and unspoken relief. Mom's hands shaking and gripping the steering wheel, and she shifted into reverse with an urgency that made the car shudder. Just as she began to pull away, a sickening sight met our eyes. Denny staggering out of the house, blood streaming from his head like a crimson river. His voice, raw and desperate, screamed through the night air.

"PLEASE DON'T GO," he yelled, hitting the car's hood, eyes wild with regret and aggravation. "PLEASE, I MESSED UP!"

Mom's face hardened, eyes cold and fierce as she screamed back through the window, "STAY THE HELL AWAY FROM US!"

The tires screeched as she peeled out of the driveway, racing down the street, the sound of the engine drowning out everything else. I turned my head and stared out the window, watching the clouds from a distance. At that moment, a quiet prayer escaped my lips, thanking God for the courage that made Tareka speak the truth. As scared as we all were, Mom taking that first step meant the world to us.

Love with Limits

Relief washed over me like a cool wave, seeping into my veins and numbing the years of dread. For the first time, I felt a sense of freedom. Mom was taking us away from this life, and there was a glimmer of hope that we could finally be safe, that we could piece back together the family we had lost somewhere in the dark. I glanced at my siblings, their faces marked with exhaustion, a look leading into an unspoken promise that we were moving toward something better.

At that moment, I knew we had survived, and Mom was the shield that would protect us, no matter what came next. The courage she had in that very moment was indescribable.

We sat huddled in the car outside Granny's house, the summer air heavy and still around us. Mom turned, her eyes sharp, slicing through the silence as she looked at our faces. Her voice, low and taut, cut through the unease.

"Don't tell Momma anything about what just happened. Do you all understand?"

We nodded, fear clinging to our words as we whispered, "Yes." The weight of her command pressed down on us, suffocating and cold. My mind raced with questions that I dared not ask. Why wouldn't we tell Granny? Didn't she deserve to know what was happening? Didn't she have the right to help us? We were always taught, what happens in the house stays in the house no matter what.

But there was no room for doubt, no space for speaking up. We kept our promise, lips sealed as the days melted into weeks. Mom never brought it up again. There were no questions, just silence. A still sense of fear lingered: *if he comes back begging, will she return?*

It was like the past had been erased, a chapter that didn't exist in our family story. What had been done was buried, never to be dug up ever again. In those days, talking about pain was forbidden; there were no safe spaces to unravel the knots. We learned to adapt, to sweep everything under the rug and keep moving forward as if the past had never happened. And so, we did quiet, broken, and bound by the things we were never allowed to speak of.

We stepped into Granny's house, each of us clutching the few bags Mom had managed to grab. The air inside was cool but heavy, filled with the musty scent of old wood. Granny's eyes, sharp and calculating, zeroed in on us as she asked, "Is everything alright, and why do you have bags in your hand?"

Mom's voice was steady but strained. "Go to the back room and put the bags away," she said, the command urgent but laced with something I couldn't place. We didn't question it. We turned and headed toward the back of the house, the sound of our feet soft against the creaking floorboards.

Mom met Granny's eyes, the silence between them thickening like smoke. "Mom, we're fine. I need to get myself together for my kids, that is all. We need to stay here for a little while if that's alright."

Granny's eyes narrowed, the kind of look that could crack a glass. She didn't believe a word Mom said, but after a long, measuring pause, she sighed. "Alright," she said reluctantly, her voice edged with impatience. "But you need to know, you can't stay long. I've got my card games, and I don't want any disturbances. You understand?"

The warning was clear, and her focus on those games was as sharp as the edge of her poker face. She didn't care about the stories behind our bags or why we'd come. She only cared about the game, the money, and the silent ritual that demanded her full attention.

Mom nodded, her expression unreadable. "Understood," she whispered, the weight of her promise hanging in the air like a threat we'd all come to understand far too well.

My granny Sharlene and Papa Majesty, who was Mom's stepfather, didn't work real jobs, but they hosted daily card games at their house to make extra money. They would stay up all night and day partying with friends, drinking, smoking, and cursing loudly. The house felt like a party spot day in and day out, plus fights often broke out over various things. During the few weeks we stayed there, we could barely sleep. Mom was gone much of the time and left us in their care, trusting them to look after us.

Granny complained a lot about Mom, calling her unfit and irresponsible. She would curse Mom out, speak badly about her, and talk about her with contempt. Granny never missed an opportunity to remind us how unwanted we were as kids. She'd yell at us, saying things like, "You all need to go back home," making us feel unwelcome in her house. She'd remind us, "It's not my responsibility to raise you all, I already raised my own kids."

Granny didn't care as much for my siblings as she did for me. As the oldest granddaughter, I was expected to do way more than my siblings, which meant I was the main one out of the room we stayed in most of our days. Granny was disciplining me as she taught me how to clean. I eventually became a house maid, cleaning the kitchen, bathrooms, coffee tables, sweeping the floors, and vacuuming carpet. She adored her coffee tables; those were the signature to her home when anyone entered. If I didn't clean the coffee table right she'd whoop me with a leather belt or whatever she could grab until I got it right. It didn't take me long to catch on.

I wiped those glass tables so long my arm felt like it was going to fall off from my body. In return, Granny would reward me with candy and give me whatever I wanted, making it clear there was a difference between us three. It felt like a strange privilege and a burden, like I had to earn her affection through labor. I felt bad for my siblings because they had to stay in the room all day as I cleaned and barely could come out for food. I would sneak in the room, give them whatever I made for the day. I knew I was able to get more.

I never wanted them to ever feel lesser than me because we all were equal. They were often left to fend for themselves, feeling like they didn't matter as much. The divide between us grew overtime, leaving them feeling unimportant, as though their efforts and presence were never enough to earn the same love and affection I received. Sometimes my siblings would ask me things like, "How come you get to leave the room?" "We have to stay here all day!" I replied, "I'm not sure." I wasn't old enough to understand the difference between loving people equally but I also knew they had feelings too.

Heartache from love

There were times when Denny would show up at Granny's house, knocking on the door with a desperate urgency that sent chills through me as soon as I saw him. Granny would always tell him she wasn't there and send him away, her voice sharp and dismissive. But on this day, the air felt electric, heavy with something I couldn't name.

I saw Mom step out the door, her silhouette framed by the dim light. Denny stood outside, watching her with an urgency that made my breath catch. The knot in our throats growing tighter each time, wanting to cling onto her as if our love could keep her from going. We ran to the window. She walked over to his car, got in, and he pulled off, tires screeching against the gravel. My heart slammed against my ribs. Why would she get in a car with him? I thought. A man who had brought nothing but pain and fear into our lives. What could he possibly say that would make her forget? The questions spun in my head like a storm. Was he lying, whispering empty promises to draw her back in, weaving false hope with every word with that same smooth, dangerous charm? I prayed in my mind, "Please lord, don't let her take him back."

A dark gnawing dread settled in my chest as the car disappeared down the road. All I felt was that nothing would ever be the same again. A few hours later, Mom returned. She told us to gather up our things because we were going back home. The words hit us like a cold slap, and time seemed to freeze for a moment. The room felt like it was closing in, the walls pressing against us as we slowly moved, our heads bowed, feet dragging. The weight of what was happening sank in with every step, a suffocating dread that choked any little hope we had building up.

We all looked at each other, then started crying and begged Mom not to take us back. She yelled, "Y'all stop all that whining." "I said get y'all stuff because we are about to go." And just like that, with our heads down, we dragged our feet to the car. We left their house without notice. Mom knew they would binge staying up for two or three days straight playing cards, gaming, and running numbers. They wouldn't have noticed we left until it was too late. While driving us back to the house, she told us, "He apologized and said he would get help." She added, "He also promised me he'd never do it again." Then she said, "He swore it wasn't like that and that you all added stuff to the story."

I said, "But Mom, my sister did not tell a story. He has been messing with us." She said angrily, "Lamika, we are not talking about this anymore it is what it is." We pulled up to the house and he was standing in the doorway like an animal hunting his prey. He wore a victory grin ear to ear knowing he had gotten away with it like he told us he would. Seeing him again made me sick to my stomach, but there was no place to go.

We got out of the car and walked toward the house, each step harder to take than the last, as if the earth was trying to pull us back. We stepped inside, our hearts racing. Nobody said a word, but we all felt the weight of the unknown, even Mom. The facade of normalcy shattered around us, but we pretended. We had no choice but to play along, even as the truth gnawed at us, a bitter reminder that this was only the beginning. We learned how to fake our way through, tiptoeing around moods and moments, never knowing what would set things off. That became our way of surviving, walking on eggshells, hoping peace would last a little longer this time.

Shattered Trust

As a child, I was haunted by a storm of emotions, fear that gripped me in the dark, confusion that clouded my thoughts, low self-esteem that made me feel invisible, and depression that weighed me down. Trust was a foreign concept, anger simmered just beneath the surface, and emotional struggles left me feeling broken inside. The shadows of feeling scared, worried, and sad about what happened. It made us act and feel confused, even if we did not always understand why things were going the way they did. The worry would seep into every corner of our lives, making school and social situations an uphill battle, leaving marks that could tag along for years.

I didn't want to go back home and thought we had a way out. It was then I realized that something was seriously wrong with my mother for taking him back, especially after everything my sister had told her and what she had witnessed with her own eyes. When you have proof, what more do you need to believe? Mom was supposed to be our shield, who kept us safe no matter what and protected us from any hurt, harm, or danger. We trusted her to be the parent God chose her to be.

A bitter seed of resentment took root in my heart, mingling with a growing fear and a gnawing uncertainty. I felt unsafe, knowing that an adult who was supposed to be trustworthy was manipulating our lives. Yet, in that fear, I found something inside me started to grow, a quiet kind of strength that helped me get through each day we had to pretend that nothing was happening.

When it all felt too heavy, I'd drift off to my happy place. In my mind, everything was bright and safe. The grass was soft beneath my feet, the sun always shined, and my laughter sounded like music. My brother and sister were there too, running beside me through wide open fields. Nobody was mad, nobody yelled. We picked wildflowers, raced the wind, and collapsed in the grass just to stare at the clouds. In that world, I didn't have to be scared or small, I could just be a kid.

It wasn't long before Denny's presence slipped back into our world, quiet but heavy, as if time had rewound itself and we were meant to relive it all over again. Denny's voice was low, laced with an edge that sent chills through my spine. "Y'all slipped up this time, but next time, I'm going to kill y'all Momma." The words hung in the air, heavy with a promise that left no room for doubt. Whenever Mom wasn't around, he would have his way with us, and the frequency grew like a dark storm, moving from once a week to four times, then nearly every day creeping his way back into what was normal. The house, once filled with laughter long ago, became an echo of silence and tension.

The arguments between him and Mom grew more volatile; their fights were now a constant thundercloud that dwelled over us. This was when he started hurting her in ways that made the air feel suffocating. We adapted, becoming numb to our surroundings, trying to hold on to whatever remnants of childhood we had left. But I couldn't stop the anger from seeping into me or the fear that clawed at my chest whenever I thought of what may happen to us next. We couldn't trust anyone anymore, not even each other. He was getting everything he wanted, leaving us with nothing to cling onto.

Peace Beyond the Clouds

When the house finally grew quiet at night, it wasn't peace, it was that uneasy kind of quiet that made our stomachs twist. My siblings and I would whisper to each other in the dark, tired and scared. "I wish he'd forget tonight." "I wish he'd leave us alone." "I hate him," we whispered, our voices barely holding together with frustration. We would ask each other questions none of us knew the answers to. My siblings would lean on me because I was the oldest, and all I could do was give them a nurturing response. I could naturally find words that offered them some hope of better days ahead. We were becoming more and more drained and exhausted.

"Please let us sleep tonight," I wholeheartedly whispered with a sigh. We'd talk about how tired we were, how we wished we could find someone to tell, someone who would listen and believe us. Someone who cared. But hope was a fragile concept, one we could no longer afford to hold onto. There was something shifting in the atmosphere that felt like a change was coming, but none of us knew whether it would be for the good or bad.

Our small bodies bore the evidence of the torment we endured: bruises that told stories too painful to share, marks that ached with every movement, and a constant soreness that became a part of our existence. Over time, our bodies grew accustomed to the pain, as if it were woven into the fabric of our being. How much would a child withstand before breaking? When would the threshold be crossed, the point where enough was enough? We had talks about fighting back or losing our lives. The questions floated through the pain.

A storm of doubt and confusion swirled in my mind. I couldn't stop thinking about how a mother, someone meant to protect her children at all costs, could choose to believe the man who hurt them. It made me question everything. Is this what love is supposed to look like? Is this how I'd treat my own kids one day? It just couldn't be. Nothing about being hurt, left alone, or made to suffer in the dark could ever be right. Sometimes I wonder if she blocked it out on purpose, if pretending not to know made it easier to live with. I don't even know what I'm supposed to feel anymore.

Am I supposed to be angry? Sad? Numb? Maybe this is what it feels like when something inside you starts to fade, when you've cried so much that the tears stop coming. The hardest part wasn't what happened; it was realizing our own mother wouldn't believe us. The walls of our world felt like they were closing in, leaving us trapped in a nightmare with no escape. We were alone, and the trauma that followed was deafening. You never know how deep childhood scars can cut, shaping your mind in ways you never saw coming.

Denny never let up, constantly inventing new ways to torment us, pushing the boundaries of what we could endure. When Mom left, he would tear the top mattress from the bed and drag it into the front room, tossing it onto the floor like an afterthought. The creak of the springs echoed in the silent house, a cruel prelude to the night ahead. He would come for us one by one, his footsteps reverberating down the hallway, cold and heavy like a death knell. Each step made my heart pound, and each shadow sent a jolt of fear through my veins.

There was no escape, no safe corner left to hide in only the suffocating darkness and the weight of a childhood lost. Silently, we had no choice but to go along with it, our minds retreating into themselves, shutting off the pain as best as I could. I found a safe space in my thoughts that was safe, somewhere far away from the horror around me. Numbness became our shield, the only defense we had left. I turned my head, squeezed my eyes shut, and willed myself to be somewhere other than here. For a while, I didn't feel anything. The pain became background noise, something I learned to live with. But somewhere deep inside, a small spark refused to die. Once I closed my eyes I went back to that place that made me feel alive again. In my mind, the air was warm, and the sky stretched wide and open. The grass was soft beneath my feet, and the laughter of me and my siblings floated in the distance. No yelling, no fear, no pretending. Just us, free and whole.

I could feel the sunshine on my face and the wind in my hair, and for the first time in a long time, I remembered what peace felt like. I hoped and prayed that these moments would come to an end, that I would finally be able to crawl back into bed and bury myself under the covers, away from the nightmares that crept through the dark. We all suffered a different kind of pain, awaiting the day Mom would see the light.

Hidden Battles Within

Most days, we didn't even understand what was happening. My mind was constantly racing, relentless and unyielding. I would always think: *Everyone's boyfriend does this to their kids. Is this what I was born for? Should I sneak away and ask someone if this was normal?* But deep down, I knew it couldn't be. The things happening to us felt like a waking nightmare, a world twisted so far from reality that I couldn't convince myself it was real. It was as if my childhood was slipping through my fingers, replaced with something dark and foreign, a life I did not want to accept. I always had a feeling that there was so much more in store for me. I felt in my heart that there had to be more to life than this.

Mom wasn't the same anymore; she hadn't been for a long time, just slipping away from the woman she once was. The days blurred together as she slept longer, stopped cooking for us, and abandoned the neatness she always took pride in. Her hair, once perfectly styled, now lay in unkempt braids at the back of her head. She went from being a mother who worked full-time to someone who barely left the house. Laundry piled up in corners, untouched and forgotten.

The food in the cabinets dwindled to a few lonely cans, and the lights flickered like they were clinging to life. Her clothes hung off her now-thin frame, and the TV antenna we once relied on vanished. We watched her waste away day by day, and the house reflected dirt and disorder seeping into every open space. Something had taken hold of her, something stronger than us, and I had no idea how to fight it or figure out what it was.

Birthdays came and went, unnoticed, each passing year blending into the next. What once felt like a celebration now felt like just another day in the silence of our home. Our small bodies ached from exhaustion, worn down from the inside out. The family began to notice our absence, the way we stopped showing up, the way we faded into shadows. Granny would come by, her voice sharp with frustration, and the arguments would erupt, loud and relentless. Mom would send us to our room, eyes cast down, hearts heavy. She'd shoo Granny away, refusing her entry as if the house itself was a secret too dark to reveal.

Moments in her right mind she'd drop us off at Granny's, and on those days, we could forget. We could run outside, feel the sun on our skin, and pretend we were just kids for a little while. It was the closest we came to normal, the closest we could breathe without feeling the weight of everything and everyone giving up on us. One day, Granny let Jefferson and me play outside. Tareka was in trouble and on punishment secluded to the room. We were running around the neighbors' car, chasing each other. We found tiny rocks on the ground, tossing them to tag each other. All of a sudden, one of the tiny rocks hit the neighbors' car window. It shattered the glass everywhere. Jefferson covered his mouth because he didn't mean to throw it at the car.

We both knew once anyone found out we would get a beating. We were so scared so we ran in the house and buried ourselves in the room with our sister hoping no one would know it was us. Our uncle Errick burst into the room and said "Owwwwwwwwww, one of y'all in BIG TROUBLE." "Who was outside playing around the car?" Jefferson and I started crying but didn't say a word. Granny knew which ones were able to play outside. Uncle Errick instantly knew it was us from our reaction. He came into the room and closed the door behind him. He whispered, "Do y'all want to know what I used to do when I got whoopings?" We both nodded our heads yes as we were both terrified for our lives.

He said, "Sneak into the bathroom one at a time and put as much toilet paper as you can in your underwear, preferably your butt area." "It is where she will whoop y'all at and stuff it until you can't stuff anymore." Uncle Errick said, "Good luck, I remember those days." Chuckling as he slid out the room unnoticed. We looked at each other and moved swiftly to execute the plan before Granny came back to the house. I went into the bathroom first and my brother right after. A few moments later, Granny came into the house furious. Our hearts beating out our chest, breathing a million seconds a minute.

Grandpa Majesty right behind her yelling, "Dina will be paying for that window because we are watching her bad ass kids." "Where is she at anyways she needs to come get them right now." Granny marched down the hallway and flung the door open. "Who hit the window with the rock?" Neither one of us owned up to it but she knew who was out there. She yelled for Majesty to grab a thick switch off a tree in the backyard. She said, "Since no one will own up to it, both of y'all getting your ass whooped." "Starting with you Lamika!" Majesty happily brought the switch to her as he was ripping the leaves off. It was huge and thick with the thorns on it. I instantly begged for forgiveness and told her it was a mistake. She raised her arm high in the sky and swung, and instantly my skin was on fire. I started jumping around in the bathroom as she kept swinging. She noticed that I wasn't screaming like I should have been. She stopped swinging and said, "Wait a minute!" "Where is all the toilet paper?" "I know I just put a full roll on there."

I shook my head saying, "I don't know Granny." "Please, I'm sorry." She yanked the back of my pants down instantly. She said, "Do you think I'm stupid or I wouldn't have noticed?" I said, "No, Granny I didn't mean too." She yelled, "Pull your pants down and take that toilet paper out of there." "When you get finished, bend over the toilet." I froze, embarrassed and scared, not sure what to do or say. My throat tightened, and my eyes burned, but I didn't let the tears fall. At that moment, I realized how small I was and how little my words meant. I just wanted it to be over.

She hit me over 10 times and did the same with Jefferson. Afterward, we didn't say much. We just sat there, both staring at nothing. It was like the air got stuck in our chests, too heavy to let out. I could tell by the way he looked at me that he didn't know what to say either. We were both embarrassed, hurt, and confused. It wasn't just the pain; it was the way it made us feel inside, like we couldn't trust the people who were supposed to love us.

That night, we didn't talk. We just laid there, eyes open, pretending to sleep. Even in the dark, I could feel his sadness matching mine, two kids trying to make sense of something that didn't make sense at all. It was hard for us to sit on our bottoms due to them being split open in areas. It took us a few days to be comfortable to sit down again. Mom came to pick us up days after, and we never spoke a word of what happened.

Mom typically left the door unlocked at home, a silent invitation to whatever darkness lay outside. It felt like the house had given up, its defenses crumbling, exposing us to whatever came next. We never knew who would walk in; sometimes, it was a neighbor or someone who shouldn't have been there. The absence of security and safety seeped into our bones, making the world feel even more dangerous. Like us, it was as if the house was waiting for something to change.

We had no stable place to call home and no school to settle into for long. Mom's struggle to keep up with the bills became too much, and then Denny's violence pushed her to her breaking point. Bruised and battered, she packed what little she could and made the decision to leave him. A ride picked us up and took us to the shelter, a lifeline for battered women, open 24 hours a day, and welcomed us with open arms. It's been a while since we felt kindness like that.

It was a place where women could heal, rebuild their lives, and move forward with dignity. They provide emergency housing, food, essential resources, counseling, legal assistance, and job training programs to help women regain independence. Mom promised that she was fighting to become the woman she once was. We held on tight, tears falling, bound by the same desperate hope that had carried us through so much of life.

When she checked us in, my siblings and I were led to a small, dim room with a single bunk. We crammed into that bed, four bodies pressed together for warmth and comfort. Meals were served like clockwork. Each morning, Mom left to look for work, her footsteps echoing down the hall a sound that meant she hadn't given up. Bit by bit, she was becoming the mother we remembered, the one we'd missed for so long.

Fighting Quiet Wars

Mom had finally enrolled us back in school, trying to piece together a sense of normal life again. I remember clutching my backpack that first morning, nerves twisting in my stomach.

I boarded the school bus with a hesitant look, bracing myself for the world waiting at the end of the ride. But the world wasn't kind.

"Look, y'all, she lives at the shelter! HA HA HA!" The laughter followed me like a shadow, loud and sharp.

"Look at her clothes and shoes, did the shelter give you those?" Kids pointed and snickered, their voices cutting through the morning air. I overheard their whispers on the ride to school.

"Kids that live at the shelter are poor. Their parents don't have any money."

I bit my lip, fighting the tears in my eyes. The bus ride felt like a journey through fire; I kept my head down, avoiding their eyes, knowing that any sign of strength would be seen as a challenge, a reason for them to push and shove me further. My heart ached, but I held it together, refusing to let them see me break. I cried silently, every insult carving deeper scars. After everything I'd already been through, my skin still wasn't tough enough for this kind of fight.

But despite it all, I was grateful. I am grateful that I woke up that morning. I am thankful that Mom was beginning to reclaim herself, piece by piece. We had a chance, a flicker of hope in the chaos. We could have a fresh start. I let my mind drift, imagining a world where those kids knew the truth, where they understood the battles we fought and what we had survived. Would they have still laughed? Or would they have seen me for the fighter I was, someone who had made it through when so many didn't?

I learned the sting of being different, the harsh whispers, the laughter as I was shoved around in the hallway. They didn't know what we'd endured, didn't know how grateful we were to have a roof over our heads, a bed, and a warm meal. They didn't see how the shelter was our sanctuary, our hope beyond all hopes, and I held onto that, even as the bullying chipped away at me little by little.

Then one day, a teacher handed me a small notebook and said, "Maybe it'll help to write things down." I didn't know it then, but that notebook became my lifeline. I started writing everything my feelings, my fears, my dreams. I wrote about my happy place, where the sun always shined and nobody was mean. I wrote about the kind of life I wanted, the goals I'd reach one day, the peace I'd create for myself and others. Each word I put on paper felt like a tiny step out of the darkness. I began to believe that maybe, just maybe, I could turn my pain into something good.

We loved our mom so much, and deep down, we believed that she would become better. She would find a way to pull herself together and lead us to a better life. Weeks turned into months, and life in the shelter felt like a fragile truce, a pause between storms. One day, after school, Mom came into the lobby with eyes so bright and full of life that it was like the sun had returned to her world. "I found a job!" she said, and her voice trembled excitedly. At that moment, her joy was contagious, like a warm light spreading to all of us. It was more than just good news; it was that piece of hope, a tangible reason to believe we might be okay. We were all so happy for her, and that night, the small space we shared seemed full of magic.

After she got her first check, she stopped by the gas station on the way home and brought us snacks, something simple, but how she handed them to us made them feel like the greatest treasure. We sat together, laughing and joking, our happiness filling the room as we soaked up the rare feeling of peace. No arguments, no angry voices, no waking up out of our sleep, no urgent need for extra baths, or the restless tossing through the night. Together, we wrapped in that delicate moment where everything felt right. It felt alright to breathe again.

That night stayed with me. It wasn't about the snacks or the laughter; it was about the feeling that maybe life could start to make sense again. For the first time in a long time, I saw a glimpse of the mother I missed, the one who smiled without pain behind her eyes. Sitting there, I realized how much I wanted moments like that to last forever. It gave me hope that healing was possible, even if it came in small, quiet ways.

Our love for Mom was unwavering, fierce, and pure. In that brief interlude, we saw her not just as our mother but as the woman who could shine brighter than any darkness. I saw a person so strong, someone who kept going no matter what. I knew she wanted to fight for something greater, to show her kids she could do it. As time went on we embraced our daily routines. The morning light cast a muted glow across the shelter's worn walls as we gathered our things, the excitement of our stay still hanging in the air. It was a rare, beautiful sight, the promise of something different, something better. The hope was electric, sparking between us like the warmth of a long-lost sun. It felt like we were each finding our path, the one meant just for us, and nothing could come between that.

Chapter Four
Consumptions of Weakness

But the whispers were there, creeping around the edges of the room. The way she stared out the window a little too long or how her fingers tapped against her leg when she thought no one was watching said something she wouldn't. We noticed, but we were too afraid to ask. Something was missing in her, like part of her mind was somewhere else. I saw it in that faraway look, the kind you get when you are trying to fill an emptiness that nothing seems to reach.

Mom's voice broke the quiet as she packed our small duffel bags with worn clothes and battered shoes. "I'll be back soon. I promise. We're almost there, I swear." Her words wavered as she tried to sound confident, but we could hear the tremor hiding underneath. She gave us one last look before stepping toward the door. We stayed inside the shelter, watching through the window as she disappeared into the cold. A few minutes passed, but she did not return. Curiosity got the best of us, so we slipped on our jackets and went to the door.

Outside, the air was biting, and the world felt bigger than it did from behind those walls. The city was alive with kids yelling, car horns blaring, and the wind cutting through our thin coats. We spotted Mom on the sidewalk, glancing down at her phone, waiting for a call or a text. Then her eyes lifted, and she froze. Standing at the corner, leaning against a lamppost, was Denny.

The sound around us faded. We did not know what she saw in him or why she could not see the danger, but the look in her eyes told us she was already somewhere else, caught between the hope she wanted and the pain she could not let go of. She was caught between the past and the present, between what was safe and what was a lie disguised as comfort.

A sudden burst of movement caught our attention as Mom ran back into the shelter. Her face was pale, and her hands trembled as she grabbed her coat from the chair by the door. Without saying much, she turned toward us, eyes darting between the window and our faces.

"Mom, don't go," I whispered, the words barely audible above the chaos of the city. My heart pounded in my chest, my siblings' eyes wide and confused. She took a breath, squared her shoulders, and turned to us with a forced smile. "I have to, kids," she said, her voice so steady it almost fooled us. "It's the only way." as her words came out soft and shaky.

We didn't know if it was for us or her, but we followed, the weight of her decision pressing down on us like the cold seeped into our bones. As we walked towards him, he pushed off the lamppost, a grin spreading across his face that made our blood run cold. As we walked, the city's noise seemed to blur, becoming nothing more than a dull roar in the background. Denny's grin widened, a flash of teeth that looked out of place in the dreary afternoon. His eyes swept over us, sharp and cold, before landing on Mom. The weight of his gaze was enough to make the hair on the back of my neck stand on end.

Mom's hand trembled as she reached out to him, her fingers brushing his arm. It was a gesture that spoke of desperation and familiarity, a plea without words. I glanced at my siblings, their eyes wide, mirroring the storm brewing inside me. We didn't want to understand it, didn't want to know why she would go back. But the questions lurked in the atmosphere, unanswered and unforgiving. Jefferson's face tightened, his fists clenched and trembling with anger he could barely hold in. Tareka stood teary-eyed, rocking gently as if her body was caught between running and breaking. It looked like she could bolt down the road and never look back. I carried the weight of disappointment on my face, a feeling so heavy it burned in my throat, like trying to swallow something bitter that refused to go down.

Denny spoke, his voice low and guttural, slicing through the air. "You're back. Good. You know it's better this way." Mom nodded, the smile she offered never reaching her eyes. "We're okay, kids," she said, but the doubt lingered in the room like smoke. It wasn't really a choice. We had been doing so well, finally having time with her at the shelter. For a little while, it felt like heaven.

I felt the first hint of fear tighten in my chest, the kind that coils around your ribs and won't let go. There was something different about this time, something I couldn't quite put into words. The air was electric, charged with an ominous certainty. I turned my head, glancing at the crowded street where people passed, oblivious to the scene unfolding. No one noticed us. No one would.

Denny's eyes locked with mine, a mix of challenge and warning. My heart pounded as the truth settled in. I had no power here, no voice. We were trapped in whatever game they were playing, and deep down I knew no one was coming to save us this time. All I could think about was getting my siblings out, finding a way to break the cycle we kept falling back into. If this was Mom's choice, then all I could do was hope she would one day see what it was costing us.

Mom's gaze fell to the ground as she let out a shaky breath. "Come on, kids," she whispered, almost to herself.

Uncertainty Clouds Hope

I knew then that things would change, that the line between hope and hopelessness was as thin and fragile as a spider's web. And as we followed her, the weight of our silence was louder than anything that had come before. The question was no longer whether we would be safe but what kind of life awaited us if we followed her back into the unknown. For a moment, the world fell away, leaving only the thundering of our hearts and the silent prayer that whatever came next, we could live through it.

Mom made the decision that shattered the fragile peace we had. We moved back into the house with Denny, the air thick with the weight of what we'd lost and the terror of what was to come. All the progress and dreams unraveled in the blink of an eye, and we were trapped in the same nightmare again.

When the world around me felt too heavy to carry, I turned to my notebook. It became the one place where I could breathe, where I could pour out everything I couldn't say out loud. I wrote about my days, my thoughts, and the small things that still made me smile. I filled the pages with pieces of my heart, both the broken ones and the ones still learning how to heal. Writing helped me stay grounded, reminded me that I still had control over my story, even when life felt out of my hands. In that little notebook, I found peace, purpose, and the beginning of my own strength.

We moved from house to house, never staying long enough to feel settled. The rhythm of our days was erratic, marked by whispered conversations about unpaid bills and hurried exits. Nights were the worst. The ache of an empty stomach wasn't something you could sleep away, no matter how tightly you curled up. Our clothes began to sag on our frames, sleeves too long, and waistbands slipping. Hunger had a way of making everything feel loose and hollow.

I noticed how my sister and brother's eyes followed me. They didn't have to say anything. I knew they were looking to me for something I wasn't sure I had. I kept my voice steady when I spoke to them, even though it wavered in my head. The bathwater was lukewarm, but I made sure it was ready for them, washing their little faces and scrubbing their tiny hands.

When it came to food, I did what I could. Sometimes, it was a can I managed to pry open with a butter knife or a crust of bread I'd saved from earlier. I'd hand it to them, watching as they ate slowly, savoring every bite. My stomach growled, but I ignored it. They needed it more than I did.

One afternoon, I decided to fix my sister's hair. She sat on the edge of the bed, her legs swinging while I fumbled with the curling iron. My hands weren't steady, but I remembered how Mom used to do it. I wrapped a strand of hair around the iron, watching it curl neatly. For a moment, I felt like I was doing something right.

But then, the iron slipped. It hit her arm, and the smell of burnt skin filled the room. She screamed, clutching her arm, and I froze. My heart pounded as I tried to think of what to do, dabbing at the burn with a damp towel. A blister started to rise, angry and red. She sobbed quietly, and I whispered apologies over and over, my voice breaking.

I didn't know how to be a mother. I didn't know how to be anything. But as I sat there, holding her hand, I realized it didn't matter. There was no one else. Whatever I didn't know, I had to figure out for them.

I put my own needs and safety aside to protect my brother and sister. I took on the burden to shield them from harm, even if it meant enduring the worst myself. Sometimes, my sacrifice was enough to keep them safe, but other times, it wasn't. There were moments when Denny wasn't satisfied, and my efforts felt like they weren't enough to stop the hurt.

"This is too much! I'm not doing this anymore!" Mom's voice rang out, high with frustration.

Denny's response was instant, his veins tightening as his voice rose, anger matching hers word for word. Their arguments were nothing new, just another storm moving through the house, but this one carried a weight that made the air thick, as if the walls themselves were bracing for what might come next. I was sitting on the porch when I heard yelling, so I got up and looked through the screen door.

I was small and unnoticed, my heart pounding in my chest. They were chest to chest now, locked in a battle of words, neither backing down. I felt the familiar flicker of fear creep up my spine, but I knew better than to interfere.

Then, it happened.

In an instant, Denny's hands shot out, and before I could process what was happening, he shoved Mom with a force that sent shockwaves through her body. She crashed into me, and together we flew backward through the screen door. The frame gave way with a sharp crack, and for a split second I was weightless, my feet lifted off the ground, then came the hard, breath-stealing impact.

I tumbled down the porch stairs, my body crashing against the solid ground below. Pain erupted through me, but all I could process was the sharp ringing in my ears and the sting of hot tears streaming down my face.

Mom's voice cut through the haze, her curses sharp as she scrambled toward me. "Lamika! Baby!" I was crying, but I didn't know why until I saw the horror in her eyes. Warmth trickled down my lips, and when I touched my face, my fingers came away slick with blood. My nose. It was broken.

I could hear Denny still yelling in the background, but at that moment, all I saw was Mom's face fear, anger, heartbreak. A mix of emotions she tried to bury, but I could see through the cracks.

She scooped me up in her arms, her hands trembling as she wiped the blood from my face. I could feel her heart pounding against mine as she rushed me out of the yard, away from the chaos, away from him.

The hospital was a blur of bright lights, the sharp scent of antiseptic, and the quiet murmurs of nurses who barely asked questions. My nose throbbed with a dull, relentless ache as they stitched me up, but the real pain sat deeper, somewhere unspoken.

And then, just like that, we were back home.

No one spoke about what happened. No whispered apologies, no angry aftermath, no questions. The house swallowed the night's violence like it had done so many times before, tucking it away in the corners where memories went to disappear. We moved on. Because that's what we were taught to do: normalize the unthinkable, silence the unbearable. And so, we did.

Broken, yet trying!

My siblings became more than just my family; they were like my own children. I would have done anything, even given my life, to protect them. Our bond grew stronger through the pain and struggles we faced together.

As time passed, Denny and Mom became less present in our lives. They would disappear for days on end, leaving us to fend for ourselves. Most days, the house was eerily quiet, with just the three of us left to figure things out. It felt like we were forgotten, abandoned to survive in a world that was far too harsh for kids our age.

The atmosphere was thick with despair as we huddled together in the small kitchen, stomachs aching and tears streaming down. Mom and Denny were just a few steps away, lying in their bedroom with the door wide open, yet it might as well have been a world apart. Their snores and silence filled the air, drowning out the sounds of hunger and desperation from the kitchen.

Tareka's cries broke the stillness first, soft but insistent. Then Jefferson joined in, his wails rising to match hers, a heartbreaking duet that echoed through the space. I stood there, helpless for a moment, feeling the weight of their need pressing down on me. I had to do something.

Determined, I climbed onto the counter, my small hands searching the cabinets with frantic energy. My eyes scanned every inch, my fingers reaching into the dark corners, hoping for a forgotten crumb, a stray cracker, anything. The cabinets were as empty as our bellies, bare shelves mocking my efforts. The sound of crying grew louder, pulling at my heart, but still, Mom didn't stir.

"Shut up in there, or y'all are gonna get an ass-whoopin'!" her muffled voice boomed from the bedroom. The threat sent a chill through me. I jumped down quickly and rushed to soothe my siblings; their tiny faces streaked with tears. "It's okay," I whispered, though I didn't believe it. I held them close, trying to quiet their cries to avoid punishment. But their hunger wasn't something I could hush away with stomachs touching our back.

Desperate, I went to the bedroom. Mom lay there, stretched out on the bed, her body unclothed and limp, her breathing steady as if nothing was wrong. "Mom, we're hungry," I pleaded softly, shaking her arm. She barely opened her eyes, muttering, "I'll feed y'all in a little bit," before turning over. Her words were empty, a dismissal meant to make me leave. I stood there for a moment, staring at her still form, wondering how she could ignore us like this. How could she not hear the cries of her children echoing just feet away?

I walked back to the kitchen empty-handed and heavier than before. My siblings looked up at me with tear-streaked faces, their cries now quieter but no less painful. I was trying to take away some of their hurt, wishing I could give them more. Wishing someone would hear us. Wishing someone would care or even notice we were there.

I spotted a can of fruit cocktail at the far back of the refrigerator's top shelf. The rusted lid shimmered faintly, a beacon of hope. I snatched it down and fumbled for the can opener, my hands trembling from exhaustion and hunger. The metal resisted, but I kept turning, desperation fueling each twist. The lid finally lifted enough for me to catch a glimpse of the sweet syrup inside.

Tareka's eyes brightened when she saw the half-open can. Rek was always impatient, always diving in headfirst without thinking twice. "I want the cherry!" Rek said, her eyes lighting up as she spotted the single bright red piece swimming in syrup, aiming for the prize. "Let me get the cherry out first." She insisted she didn't need help. But as she struggled with the jagged edges of the can, her finger got stuck under the sharp lid.

In the split second that followed, chaos erupted. Before I could stop her, her finger darted into the narrow gap. The metal rim tore off half of her finger, leaving the bone and nail bed. Time slowed as I glanced at my brother, who smiled in relief, unaware of the nightmare unfolding. Suddenly, my sister let out an ear-splitting scream that pierced through the air, sharp enough to make my heart stop. I turned just in time to see her finger split open, blood spilling down and mixing with the syrup in the can. The exposed bone was a sharp, white reminder of the danger.

I whipped my head around to see blood gushing from her tiny finger, spilling into the can like a crimson waterfall. The tip of her index finger was mangled, the skin and meat torn away to reveal the stark white of bone. My breath caught in my throat as I stared in horror, unable to move. My brother's eyes widened, tears gathering as he looked at my sister then me, his face etched with fear. The cherry sat there in the can, untouched, mocking us.

Mom's voice broke through, cutting through the horror like a knife. She appeared in the doorway, eyes wide and full of shock as she took in the sight. Without hesitation, she scooped Tareka into her arms and ran to the car, her feet pounding against the floor as they disappeared.

Jefferson sat frozen, eyes fixed on the bloodstained can. His small hands clenched tight as if holding onto the last thread of comfort. Denny took full advantage of the situation and called me into the bedroom. My heart sank as I glanced back at Jefferson, sitting in front of the flickering screen, eyes wide with confusion.

"I'll be right back," I said, barely audible. I bit down on my fear and gave my brother a shaky smile, trying to keep it together. I adjusted the TV so he could see the grainy images through the static, then stepped into the hallway and closed the door behind me.

Slither in the shadows

I learned to cope by retreating to a happy place in my mind whenever bad things happened. I'd immerse myself in memories of joyful moments with my mom, eating candy, and running around outside, smiling with my siblings. It wasn't just recalling memories; I would fully transport myself in my mind. I could smell the food my mother was cooking in the kitchen and felt my sister's hand in mine as we twirled in circles. But sometimes, my mind wouldn't go anywhere; it would become completely blank. My brain often shifted into trauma mode, detaching my consciousness from reality and my physical body to protect me from what was happening.

Mom and my sister came back from the hospital that day. Her finger was now stitched and tightly wrapped, a reminder of the accident. Mom brought food home, a rare blessing that felt like salvation. The question gnawed at me in my head: *Did someone have to get hurt for us to eat?* Deep down, I blamed myself for trying to feed my siblings, for taking that can down, and for not watching Tareka more carefully. Mom was furious, her anger sharp and blistering, a punishment I accepted with my head lowered.

Life was a chaotic blur for us as kids. We had no steady ground, no sense of what came next. Mom and Denny would get dressed up, leave, and come back fighting, a never-ending cycle of noise and anger. And when they were gone, we would wait, eyes fixed on the door, hearts heavy, hoping she would return before the night swallowed us whole. Sometimes, we played in the leaves scattered in the front yard, pretending to be safe while the door stood unlocked behind us, an unguarded passage to whatever waited outside.

Some nights, Mom would arrange for family members to watch us. One of them was our big cousin, Nazario. He was a familiar presence from small gatherings, a heavyset teenager around 13 years old. When Mom left for the night, the house was quiet except for the low hum of the television in the front room. Mom ended up leaving the house and he would volunteer to come watch us, while she was gone.

Suddenly, the floorboards creaked beneath heavy steps, sending a jolt through the air. Nazario had crept into our room, the weight of his steps sending tremors through the floor. We lay still, half asleep, finding it hard to rest. We felt the shift in the air when he sat down at the end of the bed.

My sister, closest to the light switch, stirred, half-awake and scared. "What do you need or want?" she said, trembling.

"I want you. Come here," he said, the words low and cold. He reached for her feet, his touch brushing against her leg.

She yanked her leg away, scooting as far from him as she could, the thin blanket clutched to her chest. She didn't say a word, and the room fell back into a suffocating silence as he left, his heavy footsteps fading into the front room.

I blinked awake for a split second; my breath caught in my throat as I realized what had just happened. Questions haunting me: *People had to see the fear in our eyes. Did anyone know the pain we carried, or did they just see an opportunity?* So many questions lingered in the dark, unanswered and heavy.

I whispered a prayer into the quiet, asking God to protect me and my siblings from any more harm, hurt, or danger.

As kids, we learned early that no one would believe us, or worse they'd say it was our fault. Was it normal to stay silent, to never address the darkness that shadowed us? We didn't talk about it, not to each other or Mom, who already carried so much on her own. We loved her too much to let her take that burden, so we kept quiet, even when the silence choked us. Things just happened, and we went with the flow.

I knew something was wrong with Mom. There were nights when her eyes seemed lost, and she'd stare into the distance as if searching for a past that had slipped through her fingers. But the details were a mystery, and questions had no place in our world. We were children trying to survive, our minds too young to grasp the complexities of what was happening.

I often wondered: was it wrong of me, the oldest, to remain silent? Could I have changed things and stopped some of what we went through? The weight of responsibility pressed on me like a storm cloud, relentless and suffocating. My mind battled the guilt, the confusion of what was right or wrong in moments when the choices seemed too big for our little lives. We fought wars we weren't supposed to in a world where we had no allies, no safety net—only for each other and an unspoken trust in God, who became our only refuge.

But yet still, the questions continued eating away at me: *Does everything happen for a reason, or is that just something people say to make sense of chaos? Would we ever find the peace we deserved, or would we carry the echoes of these moments forever?* Denny hasn't been home in a while, maybe they are finally done.

Life flows within

In the late '80s and early '90s, televisions weren't what they are now. Forget remotes with batteries or Alexa to control the screen. Recording shows? Setting timers? That was futuristic nonsense. We relied on a perfectly good index finger to push a square button to turn the TV on and off. Adjusting the volume? That required two working fingers to pinch a gray knob and twist it just right. The bigger knob next to it controlled the channels, but with only 13 to choose from, the odds of finding something better than static were slim. And those long, wiry antennas? They demanded patience, twisting them every which way in a 360-degree ballet to clear up the blurry picture. One of my heartfelt memories was standing in front of a gray-screen television with my siblings, Tareka and Jefferson. I was the tallest, my sister came next, and then my brother, whose big head made him look like he was carrying a globe on his tiny shoulders.

In addition, when it was us against the world, our morning ritual never fell short. We were like clockwork. We'd tumble out of bed, rub the sleep from our eyes, and turn on the TV before we did anything else. Our mission? To catch "I Like Big Butts" by Heavy D. I couldn't help but wonder what kind of name was "Heavy D" anyway. The name fit perfectly; he was heavy, and his name started with a D. That was logical enough in my little brain. He was so big, yet somehow, all the skinny women in the video adored him, which made my little self think he must've been special. I wish we had someone to adore us all the time. I noticed we were missing more than we gained.

We'd belt out the chorus like we were on stage, my sister and I taking the lead while Jefferson took on the man's verse. Poor Jefferson didn't know the words, but that didn't stop him. He'd mumble incoherently, his little body swaying to the music with his oversized head bobbing back and forth like it had a mind of its own. We couldn't help but giggle. It took all his energy he had just to carry that head around, and here he was, swinging it like a pro. When he stumbled or froze mid-verse, my sister and I swooped in, harmonizing to save the song like the backup singers we imagined ourselves to be.

Our bond was as solid as that ancient TV. We didn't need cable or cartoons, nor could Mom afford them. All we needed was each other, a catchy tune, and the kind of laughter that echoed outside the house's walls and followed us into our dreams. Every day began and ended with the three of us wrapped in the kind of joy that didn't come from a screen but from the love we carried for each other.

Sometimes, it takes a moment to realize life is not as it should be. All children need is love and affection from the people who brought them into the world. But what happens when that love is replaced by silence, neglect, and the cold shadow of abandonment? We didn't deserve to be left alone, ignored, or afraid.

I started journaling to help find my strength again. Even though I couldn't open up to another anyone, I began writing everything down: my thoughts, my pain, my hopes on anything I could find to write on. Each word I wrote helped me see myself a little clearer. Slowly, I started to feel the weight lift. I began learning how to love myself instead of doubting who I was, reminding myself that I didn't do anything wrong. Writing became my way of healing, one page at a time.

I knew that when I grew up, I wanted to help people. I held on to positive phrases and little reminders that the ending could be brighter than the beginning. I would hear small positive words that I often repeated from the TV screen commercials. I made a promise to myself that everything I endured wouldn't be in vain. One day, the pain I carried would become the reason someone else found hope, healing, and the courage to keep going.

Ticking of the clock

We needed to get Mom back, but she wouldn't wake up. There were days when it felt like we were in a race against time. It wasn't like how we remembered her. Instead, sometimes, she just stayed in bed. No matter how many times we called her name or shook her gently, she wouldn't respond. It felt like she was somewhere else, far away, and we didn't know how to reach her.

We didn't understand exactly why. We were too young to know all the details. It was like her body was there, but her mind or spirit wasn't. So, we had to do anything to bring her back to us, even if it felt strange or extreme. My siblings and I constantly thought about her. We all worried ourselves even as she slept.

One time, my sister came to me with huge, frightened eyes, whispering, "Mom's dead, sissy." My heart clenched as we rushed into her room, screaming her name and shaking her as if we could bring her back. But there was nothing, no response, no sign she was still there.

She had a determination that belied her small frame. She would grab a cup of water, cold and sharp, and throw it in Mom's face. In her young mind, it was a silent plea: *Get up. Be here. Take care of us.* Mom's eyes would snap open like she was breaking the surface of the water, gasping for breath as if waking from a nightmare. But even then, her movements were sluggish, her presence hollow.

But this strange feeling came with it like we were trying to fix something we didn't understand. Why wasn't she awake already? Why did we have to throw water on her? And yet, somehow, it worked. She'd get up, groggy and grumbling, but she was there again. It's not perfect, but here, at the moment, we are with each other. I didn't know why she was so distant sometimes, but when we did things like this, I just hoped it would bring her back and bring us back.

Mom started doing weird things like eating the ashes from her cigarettes, a desperate habit that made our stomachs turn. All night, she would stay awake, drifting in a fog we couldn't interfere with. And when morning came, she would sleep again, wrapped in the exhaustion that seemed to drain her of life. We didn't understand it. She was not the woman we knew, the mother who once laughed with us, who once had a light in her eyes that made everything seem safe.

But now, we were left in the dark, trying to make sense of a mother who was no longer herself. We watched her slip further away, a stranger in the body of the person we loved. The silence between us grew heavy, punctuated only by our whispered fears and the sound of the night swallowing everything else.

Later that night, the house was draped in silence, the only sound coming from the static-riddled television, its gray-and-white screen flickering like the pulse of a weak heartbeat. My siblings and I sat in front of it, eyes fixed on the fuzzy shapes that danced across the screen, pretending the chaos outside couldn't reach us. But we were wrong.

Dread of what's next

Mom burst open the front door with such force that it slammed against the wall. Her eyes were wild, big with a fear I'd never seen before. Blood trickled down her right thigh, painting a dark, ominous trail that made my stomach turn. She staggered into the room, her voice raw and frantic.

"Get on the ground! Now!" she yelled, her voice cracking under the weight of panic.

We scrambled, throwing ourselves down on the floor, hearts pounding as we tried to understand what we saw. Mom's hands were shaking, and her face was pale and glistening with sweat. She looked like a hunted animal, cornered and desperate.

"Mom?" I whispered, my voice so small it felt like it would be swallowed by the fear taking over the room.

But she didn't answer. She moved to the phone, dialed with trembling fingers, and pressed it to her ear. The seconds stretched into an eternity before Grandma Sharlean's voice answered on the other end. In seconds, a big truck with flashing lights and a loud siren stopped in front of our house, and I felt scared because I didn't know why it was there. I watched as Mom's expression shifted from terror to a brief, fragile relief as she spoke. A trail of blood from her leg followed her to the truck. Within moments, they were at our door, pulling us into the night, leaving behind the cold, quiet house that had once been our refuge.

That night at our grandparents' house, I lay wide awake, staring at the ceiling, the echo of Mom's scream still ringing in my ears. I overheard the adults' voices, hushed but urgent, talking in the kitchen. "She ran from the drug dealer," they said. "Went to his house to pay him, and he started shooting. She tried to hide, but one of the bullets hit her leg." My siblings were fast asleep after the long day, and I was thankful they didn't hear them.

I didn't understand everything but felt the truth in the air. I'd remember Mom always being strong, invincible in the way only moms could be. She was wasting away in front of us, already fragile, weak, and breaking before our eyes.

A few days later, she came home from the hospital, pale and limping, but she still had that look in her eyes, the same one that made her seem like she was stronger than anything. We watched her carefully, our eyes following her every move. I remember holding my breath as if, if we blinked, she might disappear again. It felt like we had to be extra quiet, like even the smallest sound might make her vanish, just like the way things had been before. I didn't want to believe she was really back, even though I could see her standing before us.

It didn't take long before the outside had called her back, and the house fell silent once more, haunted by the memory of that night. The fear we felt then stayed with us, a secret we could never share, a truth we kept buried deep in the dark corners of our hearts.

Mom's absences were like an endless void that swallowed the house whole. There were days when she'd disappear for hours, sometimes days, leaving us to fend for ourselves. When she was there, her presence was like a storm moving through the house, unpredictable and unsettling. I'd hear the bathroom door creak open and close, her footsteps echoing as she paced behind it. We'd knock, scream, and beg for her to come out, our voices hoarse from crying. But she never answered, head nodding off on the toilet.

Strength feels Distant

A darkness she kept hidden was taking over her. When she finally emerged, eyes bloodshot and movements unsteady, she tried to pull herself together. She would sweep the floors with a vacant look, cook us meals made from nothing but scraps, and attempt to fix our hair even though she hadn't taken the time to wash us. We'd watch her, part terrified and part desperate for a hint of the mother she once was.

Then she'd collapse, her body surrendering to exhaustion. We'd hear her breathing slowly, see her shoulders rise and fall as she drifted asleep, only to wake like nothing was wrong. We never spoke of it, never asked her what was wrong. We were too young, too scared to understand the truth behind the mask she wore. All we knew was that whatever it was, it was consuming her and us along with it.

Our house wasn't much, just a small, two-bedroom space with a kitchen, a cramped dining area, and a tiny family room. You could see almost everything from the front door, like the house was too shy to hide its secret moments. For us, it became a world to explore. With no toys or distractions, searching every corner for something to do was a daily adventure. Being out of school again took a toll.

Mom always carried her purse everywhere, even when she slept. That bag held a strange kind of allure for us, almost like it was a treasure chest. We would tiptoe over, careful not to wake her, and rummage through it. She loved candy, and finding a piece felt like striking gold. I'd break it into three uneven pieces and hand them to my siblings, each savoring the tiny morsel like a feast.

We all shared one room, crammed into a single bed while Mom had the other. There wasn't space for luxuries like dressers, just a closet and enough room to navigate without tripping over each other. Hunger was a constant. Sometimes, drinking faucet water until our bellies felt full was the only option we had.

During one of those purse raids, I found some strange small, wiry gray pieces that looked like they came from a dish scrubber. Alongside them were broken glass pipes, their edges glinting menacingly in the dim light. I picked up one pipe and sniffed it; the acrid stench of burnt smoke made my nose crinkle. The pipe's mouth was ringed with black, scorched residue.

I didn't understand what they were, but I knew they didn't belong in a house with kids. Those objects would show up everywhere on tables and under the couch. Yet, Mom never seemed to notice we dug through her things. To us, the candy we sometimes found was worth the risk, a tiny sweetness in an otherwise bitter world.

Desperation has a way of making even the most ordinary streets feel like hunting grounds. We'd step outside, scanning the neighborhood like detectives, hoping to spot some kid playing outside. We played with anyone willing to play with us, no questions asked. Kids who barely knew our names became our best friends for the afternoon if they'd run in the yard with us or play tag down the street. We weren't picky.

The loneliness of being stuck in that small house was unbearable, and we craved connection almost as much as we craved food. The playful laughter hid the quiet desperation in our minds. Our stomachs felt like they were caving in, and our smiles masked the ache gnawing at our insides. We'd play games just long enough to scope things out. Was there a chance we'd be invited inside? Could we smell food cooking or see a parent in the kitchen?

Despite the shame, there was an odd sense of relief. Being home alone, even starving, felt safer than the alternative. No predators, no fear of harm just us, trying to make it through another day. Denny was coming and going as he pleased, slipping in and out of our lives without warning. Sometimes, he'd be gone for months at a time. The walls of the house breathed easier without him there. Other times, he'd return long enough to convince Mom or himself that he was staying, only to disappear again before she even had a chance to notice he was missing.

In those moments, we clung to each other and the tiny victories we managed to scrape together. If luck was on our side, an adult might offer something small: a sandwich, a bag of chips, or even a piece of fruit. We'd take whatever we could get, savoring each bite as if it were a feast. If no food were offered, we'd strategize, spinning little stories to the grown-ups at the door. "Our mom sent us over to borrow something for dinner," or "We're out of bread, and she told us to ask you." Sometimes it worked; sometimes it didn't.

To Live is to Suffer

Mom wore her welcome out by dropping us off at our grandparents' house. It felt like we spent more time being left with strangers than actually being with her. Sometimes, she'd disappear for hours. Other times, it was the whole day or night. I never understood why she would do this, but part of it was because she felt guilty leaving us alone at home. Whatever the reason, it always left me feeling tense and abandoned.

One evening, Mom got up out of bed like it was a special trip. "Come on, y'all, let's take a quick ride," she told us. We followed her, hoping it would be one of those rare moments to spend some quality time together. We all piled into the car. I didn't know where we were going, but I could tell by her tone that it wasn't just a regular errand. The vehicle hummed as she drove through the familiar streets, but then she turned down an alley. The street lights barely lit the way, and the buildings around us looked cold and distant. This is a new location, and it feels unfamiliar to me, like stepping into a place I've never been before. Every corner seems strange, and the atmosphere makes me uneasy, as if I don't belong here.

We stopped behind a garage in the alley of a large, old white house. Its many windows reflected the dim streetlight. The house looked like it had been here forever, with its paint peeling and the porch sagging just a little.

Mom said very little during the ride; it was a silent ride there as if she were on a mission. "OK, y'all, we're here. Let's get out and go in," she said, her voice cutting through the air. We hesitated for a moment, unsure, but we followed her anyway, stepping out of the car and into the strange surroundings.

As we started walking up to the house, I looked at my siblings, but they didn't seem to understand why this place felt different. Mom said, "This is one of my friends," but her voice didn't have the usual comfort it usually did. It felt like she was trying to convince herself more than us.

She knocked on the door, and a man answered. He was short, with thickened bones and a solid frame. His skin was pale, almost ghostly white, and his features looked hardened. I couldn't place it, but something about him didn't sit right with me. "Hey there," he greeted Mom with a smile that didn't quite match the sharp sparkle in his eyes.

We stepped into the house, and I immediately noticed the overwhelming smell of stale cigarettes and smoke from the ashtray. There were ashtrays in every corner of the room, each filled with burned-out butts, some still smoldering, some long extinguished but leaving their scent lingering in the air. It was so thick it made my throat tighten. I didn't like being in a place that smelled like this. I just wanted to leave, but Mom had other plans.

"This is NePaul," she said. "These are my kids." She rattled off our names one by one. I didn't know what to say. We were supposed to say something, but I couldn't speak. So, we all mumbled a soft, fearful "hi" to him, unsure what else to do. He didn't seem to care about our nervousness. His eyes didn't change; they were empty as if he was used to making people uncomfortable.

Mom turned to us as though everything was normal. "Y'all go upstairs and play while me and him talk," she said. It wasn't a suggestion. It was an order. We didn't have a choice, so we just went along. We trudged up the narrow staircase that creaked beneath our feet. The hallway at the top was dim, the only light coming from a small lamp on the wall. We pushed open a door into a small room with an old TV sitting in the corner. It was so quiet and we could tell no kids had been in this house for a while.

We sat on the floor, trying to pretend we weren't scared, but the silence felt heavy. I could hear footsteps downstairs, then the door shutting. A chill ran through me as I realized she left us with him. I didn't know who this man was, and I didn't know what Mom was up to in order to leave us alone with him. My mind raced and I couldn't make sense of this.

I wanted to ask questions, but I couldn't. I just sat there, watching the dust swirl in the dim light, feeling like something wasn't right but not knowing how to stop it.

Fear of Unknown

I crept out of the room, tiptoeing down the first three steps just enough to squat and peek my little head around the corner to see if Mom was still there. Plop. My body went weak, sinking heavily onto the hard, brown wooden stair, feeling the weight of everything sad, depressed, angry, and disappointed all at once. It was like I couldn't escape the heaviness pressing on my chest. I felt my mouth watering, that bitter, sour taste rising, but I covered my mouth quickly before anything could come up. The feeling was overwhelming; I just wanted to escape it all, but I couldn't. I was stuck in this place, trapped in the emotions that swelled around me.

Shaking my head in disarray and fear, I couldn't understand it. Thoughts taunted me: *Mom, where are you? Mom, why do you keep doing this to us? Why are you trusting us with strangers?* I couldn't understand why she continued leaving us in these predicaments. My mind raced with questions, none of which had answers. What is so important out there that you have to constantly leave us behind?

It felt like she was choosing everything else over us, over being with her own kids. Or wherever she's going, kids definitely can't be a part of it. But why have children if they can't go with you? That question echoed in my mind louder than the others. If we weren't a priority, why bring us into the world in the first place? Why have kids if you're going to leave them behind time and time again? It didn't make sense, and it cut deeper every time I wondered what was so important out there that it couldn't include us.

Each time, I felt more abandoned, more alone, and it hurt deeper than words could express. A wave of dismay washed over me. I felt it deep in my chest. Mom had just sent us upstairs to distract us. I wouldn't shake the feeling that she was gone. NePaul must've noticed me staring, looking for her, because he called me downstairs. My stomach churned as I hesitated, but I slowly made my way down, my feet heavy on the stairs. I needed answers.

He started talking as soon as I reached the bottom. "You're looking for your mom, aren't you?" he asked. I nodded, too scared to say anything at first. "Yes, I am. Do you know where she went?" Looking around the recliner he sat in, I hoped she had just gone to the bathroom and hadn't really left us with him. Maybe she'd come back any minute, and everything would return to normal. But deep down, I knew that wasn't likely.

"She'll be right back to get y'all," he answered. My heart hit the floor; I'm sure from the expression on my face that he could tell I felt lost and forgotten on the inside. Every ounce of my pain seemed to show, and I couldn't hide it. It was like all the feelings I had buried deep inside finally spilled out, and I was too vulnerable to mask them. The emptiness I felt was so raw and evident that I couldn't escape it, no matter how hard I tried. I wasn't sure if I believed him. My mind was racing, wondering where she was.

She snuck out without saying goodbye, and a panic washed over me. What if I never see her again? The thought hit me like a cold wave, and my heart started faster in a panic. *We can't stay here.* My mind spiraled into an angry mode. I thought anything could happen to her, and our family wouldn't even know where we were. The fear of the unknown gripped me, suffocating me. I couldn't shake the feeling that we were completely alone, lost in a place where nobody would come looking for us.

She knew. She knew we would beg her not to leave us. She knew we would cling to her like white on rice, holding on with everything we had, not wanting to let go. She knew we couldn't feel comfortable without her, that we were nothing without her presence. But she still left. I could feel it in my bones she knew exactly how much it would hurt and how much we needed her, yet she walked away. It was like she could read our hearts, like she understood the ache, the fear, and the emptiness that would settle inside us the moment she was gone. But she left anyway.

"Do you know where she went?" I pressed, needing something more concrete. "She just made a quick run. Don't worry, I won't bite," he said, his voice too smooth. I didn't like the way he said that. It made my skin twitch. He tried to distract me with something else, but his voice was a little too sweet. "Do you like candy? I have candy." He said, lingering on the word candy, like I was desperate for it. I hesitated but finally answered, "Yes, can I get some for my brother and sister too?" I didn't want to leave them out or have them come down here to get it from this stranger.

Chapter Five
Coming is a Change

> *Jefferson and Tareka were so nonchalant, not a care in the world, just watching TV. They had no idea Mom had left us there and made a run. They didn't feel the unease I felt, the gnawing worry that something wasn't right. They were just content, unaware of the fear that was building inside me. "No, they can come get their candy," he said, his tone changing. Then he said something that made my stomach twist even tighter. "Come over here and sit on my lap. I'll give you some candy."*

I shook my head, panic flooding me. "No, they can come get their candy," he said, his tone changing. Then he said something that made my stomach twist even tighter. "Come over here and sit on my lap. I'll give you some candy."

I shook my head, panic flooding me. "No, I don't want the candy." I didn't care about the candy anymore. I just wanted to get away from him. "I'm going to check on my brother and sister," I said, turning and running back up the stairs. I didn't stop running until I was back upstairs, heart pounding, trying to calm myself. I knew something wasn't right, and I wouldn't let him get close to me. But just as I thought I was safe, I heard him call for Tareka to come downstairs. My stomach dropped again. What was he going to do to her?

She was more outgoing than I was. She was always the one to chat with people, easily drawing them in, while I kept to myself more. I was more extroverted, and she was introverted. As I saw her head downstairs, I leaned closer and whispered urgently, "Don't take the candy if he offers it." But my words didn't seem to register. Her mind was fixed on one thing: the candy. She didn't look back, completely oblivious to my warning, and disappeared down the stairs.

I peeped into the room on Jefferson to make sure he was alright and safe. Before I knew it, I snuck downstairs. I saw her laughing, sitting on his lap with candy in her hand. My stomach tightened as I saw him acting strangely, adjusting in his seat, hands flowing freely on her skin and licking his lips. I couldn't shake the feeling of déjà vu, the all-too-familiar situation we had found ourselves in repeatedly; only the faces and places were different.

Suddenly, he scooted my sister over to one leg, bouncing her up and down. He reaches down, adjusting his pants, and persuades her to do the unthinkable for more candy. I felt sick to my stomach, a twisting ache that wouldn't let up. Watching what he was doing to her was unbearable. Anger surged through me not just at him for his vile actions, but at her, too. I had warned her. Don't fall for it. But she didn't listen, and it crushed me. Still, I had to remind myself that she was younger than me, with her own mind, and couldn't fully fathom the danger.

Defeated, I went back to the room and lay on the floor, staring at the ceiling. Every second felt heavier than the last. I couldn't wait for her to come back upstairs so I could tell her, *Don't you ever do that again.* But before I could act, she refused his attempts and commands, and in response, he sent her away. He called Jefferson down.

I was so drained, so emotionally exhausted, that I dozed off without realizing it. The next thing I knew, Tareka was shaking me awake, her voice panicked. "Mommy's not waking up again," she said, piercing through my grogginess.

I scrambled to my feet and rushed to check. She was lying in NePaul's bed, still as a statue. Before I could process what to do, my sister went to her goal and grabbed a cup of water from who knows where. SPLASH! She dumped it all over her face. My sister had some underlying resentment and this was her way of making mom feel it.

Mom shot up instantly, sputtering and startled, her confusion quickly becoming irritated. She didn't say much as she got dressed and took us back home like everything was normal.

But that wasn't the end of it. We visited NePaul's house a few more times over the weeks and each visit he had the same mission. He'd try his games, see who would fall for it, and then go his merry old way like his actions didn't leave scars. Each time, my anger grew at him, the situation, and even the world for allowing people like him to exist. The unspeakable moments with NePaul were buried deep with everything else, pushed aside by the fear of what revealing them might mean.

I found a piece of scrap paper and started writing down the feelings that wouldn't stop circling in my head. I wrote about being left behind, about hurt that didn't have a name, and about feeling unseen when all I wanted was to be loved right. The pencil shook in my hand, but once the words started to come, I couldn't stop them. Each word felt like a little piece of the heaviness lifting off me. Writing became my way of breathing again. For a few minutes, I felt lighter, like someone was finally listening, even if it was only the scrape paper.

Rain Before the Sun Shines

Is it normal to bury the horrible things that happen to you? To push them so deep inside that you start to believe they never existed? We never talked about our experiences, not with each other or anyone else. We didn't question the details or try to make sense of the chaos. And we never told Mom about what we endured with NePaul. It could have been the fear of disbelief or the fear of vanishing without a trace because we truly did not know what he was capable of.

We loved her too much, even after everything, to risk breaking what little pieces of her were left. We spared her feelings, like kids often do when they want to protect their parents, even if it costs them their own. Things just happened, and we went along with it, like passengers in a storm, too scared to grab the wheel.

Was I wrong for staying silent? For being the oldest and not speaking up? Could I have stopped some of the things that happened to us? These questions haunt me on a daily basis. As a child, your mind is a battlefield, constantly questioning what's right and wrong, what's safe, and what will make things worse. We fought battles that didn't belong to us. We carried weights too heavy for small shoulders to bear. We endured things no kid should ever have to endure while pretending to be okay because that's what we thought we had to do.

Does everything really happen for a reason? Or is that just something people say to make sense of the senseless? I don't know. I just know it hurts. NePaul was transporting Mom to various places, his red pickup truck serving as her makeshift chauffeur. We'd sit in the truck with him, waiting, always waiting. But tonight? This night was burned into my memory like a bad dream I wouldn't be able to shake.

NePaul pulled up to another strange, unfamiliar house, its shadowy outline making it feel even more unsettling. "Come on, y'all," Mom said. We followed, climbing into the front seat and squeezing into the space between NePaul and Mom. I looked around my siblings to see her clutching her purse and shaking her leg.

When we pulled up to the house, she turned to us and said, "Ok, I'll be back." There was no explanation, just her usual words that hung heavy in the air. We watched as she walked up to the house, her figure disappearing through the front door.

We waited. Hours passed, and the night grew colder. The windows fogged up from our breath as we sat in silence, growing restless. Eventually, exhaustion took over, and we dozed off, curled up in awkward positions against each other.

The sound of a loud engine shattered the silence, jerking us awake. A massive, white tank-like truck pulled up, its blinding lights cutting through the darkness. The air seemed to freeze as a swarm of police officers spilled out, shouting commands we couldn't make out.

My eyes widened in horror as they surrounded the house, their movements like a well-rehearsed dance. They had a battering ram, slamming it into the front door with brutal force over and over again, the sound echoing in the still night.

And then, chaos. People started pouring out of the house like water through a broken dam. They leaped from windows, scrambled down the roof, and darted through the backyard. Bodies scattered in every direction, desperate to escape the police closing in on all sides. It was like watching a swarm of panicked roaches scattering under a light, their fear palpable even from where we sat.

I pressed my face against the cold glass of the truck window, my heart pounding so loud it drowned out the noise outside. My only thought: Where is Mom? I scanned every figure, every shadow, every movement, hoping, praying I'd see her.

For us, witnessing an ambush like this wasn't just scary, it was soul-crushing. The chaos, fear, and uncertainty marked me in a way I couldn't erase. We were just kids, and yet, at that moment, it felt like we had grown old too fast.

We instantly start crying, our hearts pounding in fear. "Mom, NO! Please don't leave! Stay here. She will come out, wait…wait!" NePaul didn't even pause to check the aftermath. Without a word, he sped off down the street. We were in a sea of distress and helplessness. We watched as the lights of the truck faded, the hope of seeing our mom slowly slipping away with it. We could only pray she would come out soon, praying she was okay, that she'd be back, that we hadn't just lost her all over again.

We got out of the car, went inside, and stayed silent. I guess he could see how shaken we were, so for once, he didn't try any of his candy tricks. Hours passed, and the emptiness sank deeper and deeper into our chests. The silence was unbearable, each minute stretching longer than the last. We waited, but it felt like the world was moving on without us. Then, just as we were about to lose hope, a sound came to the front door knocking. BOOM! BOOM! BOOM!

Sprinkle of Hope

My heart dropped, and I rushed to the top of the stairs to see who it was. "Who is it?" NePaul asked. "It's me," Mom answered, her voice barely noticeable outside the door. She walked in, telling NePaul she'd just gotten out of lock-up, caught with some stuff. I broke down immediately. The worry I'd been carrying all night spilled over. I crept into the room and told my siblings, "She's at the door." We all gathered in a group hug, the weight of our fear lifting just a little as we cried together.

Mom went over to the bottom of the stairs, her eyes searching the top, waiting for our little bodies to come running down, smiling, eager to see her. "KIDS!" she yelled. She was just as happy to see us as we were to see her, but the way she stood at the bottom of the stairs, waiting, made it feel different. She didn't run up to grab us and hold us tight like she used to. She just stood there, her expression soft but not as filled with excitement. It was as if she had waited so long for this moment that she couldn't quite bring herself to rush into it.

We ran so fast that it felt like the ground beneath us was nothing but air. We grabbed her and squeezed her with everything we had. The tears of relief and joy came without warning, flowing so freely that we could hardly breathe. Every moment with her felt so precious like we could lose her again at any second. NePaul handed Mom some cash and dropped us off at home.

The days that followed blended into a familiar routine. Mom was still gone at night, and the sleepless nights of hunger became all too common. It was as if this constant absence, this gnawing emptiness, had woven itself into the fabric of our lives. We had learned to live with it, adjusting to a world where we didn't know when she'd come back or what we'd have to endure while she was gone. It became a part of us, like a shadow we couldn't escape.

Life felt like a constant rollercoaster for us. Most days, we didn't know if we were coming or going. The fear of not knowing whether she was alive or dead weighed so heavily on me. It was the reality we lived in. I was suddenly awakened one night by a loud banging on the front door. I rushed to Mom's room, but no one was there. Panic set in as I ran to the front and peered through the blinds.

It was Grandpa Majesty standing on the porch. "Lamika, it's me! Open the door!" he mumbled. I opened it quickly, and he asked, "Where's your brother and sister?" "They're sleeping in the room," I said, still groggy and confused. He looked at me firmly and said, "Grab some clothes for you all, and come with me."

He didn't give me a chance to question it. We were whisked away in the middle of the night, and when we arrived at his house with granny, he told us to go into the back room and lie down. We were so confused. Why were we being taken in the middle of the night? What was going on?

The next morning, he woke us up and sent us on our way to school. I asked, "Where's Mom?" Grandpa's face softened a little, but his tone was serious. "I'll let your Granny tell you about that." I went to school, but I couldn't concentrate. All I could think about was Mom. What had happened to her? Where was she? My heart felt heavy. We missed a lot of school and it became foreign language to us. Every time I returned to school out of nowhere, the students thought I was a new student.

When I got back to Granny's house, I couldn't wait to ask. "Where's Mom?" She looked at me with a sigh and said, "Your mom is locked up. I'll be taking care of y'all until she gets out."

The Words that Go Unheard

A few days passed, and Mom still hadn't come to pick us up. Granny, though, had begun to notice the change in us. She saw the sadness and quietness that had replaced the laughter and carefree energy we once had. Something was wrong, and deep down, Granny knew we weren't telling anyone what had been happening. She could feel it in her heart something was off, and we were holding it in.

After about a month, Mom finally came to Granny's house to take us back. But this time, Granny had a plan. She called me and my sister to the kitchen table. Mom pacing back and forth from the kitchen to the living room, her steps uneasy, as if she knew this moment was coming.

"Momma, you're crazy," Mom said. "Please don't do this, Momma." My sister and I sat across from each other, our eyes wide with uncertainty. We had no idea what would happen, but we knew it wasn't good.

Then came the question that broke everything open. Granny's voice was steady but concerned as she asked, "Has he touched y'all? Has he put his hands where they do not belong? What's been going on over there?"

My sister and I couldn't look up. We stared at the floor, tears welling up in our eyes. We didn't know what to say. We didn't know how to answer, but we knew we couldn't. If we told the truth, our lives would be in jeopardy. We couldn't risk it too much. Mom's response cut through the silence: "Y'all don't pay momma no attention," she said, trying to dismiss Granny's questions. But we couldn't ignore it anymore. The truth was starting to surface.

I'm thinking in my head that if I say anything, we all could possibly die. My feet dangled from the dining room chair, my body frozen in fear. Mom and Granny were still going back and forth, arguing. Mom defended herself, saying Denny didn't do anything, and

Granny pushed harder, insisting that something wasn't right. Every question that came from Granny made my heart pound harder:

- "Did Denny touch y'all?"
- "Did he do anything to y'all?"
- "Tell me what he did! I won't tell a soul, trust me."

My sister and I kept crying, not knowing what to do. My mind was racing, spiraling with thoughts. Tareka had already told Mom, but she didn't believe her. She went right back to him, with no hesitation. It made me sick to think about it. Why hadn't she believed us? Was this our fault somehow? Maybe if I told Granny, something would finally happen to him, but would it? What if it made everything worse?

After five long hours of being interrogated, I finally whispered, "Yes, Granny. He has been touching us."

Granny's eyes went black. "What? What did you say?" she asked, her voice shaking.

I couldn't hold it in anymore. The tears falling like oversized rain drops down my face and neck. "Yes, Denny messes with us all the time," I managed to choke out.

Granny's face went from shock to utter heartbreak. I could see her eyes transition from anger to sadness, the realization settling in. She looked at me, and for the first time, I saw her deep, profound hurt. She didn't want to believe it, but there it was.

She started crying, screaming, and yelling, "I knew it, I knew it. I could feel it! You knew this whole time, and you let him do that to your children? What type of mother are you? How could you let him do this to them? Why, Dina? Why? What has gotten into you? Are you crazy?"

Mom rushed up to me, her hands grabbing my shoulders, shaking me back and forth. "Tell her you never told me about it! Tell her!"

I couldn't say anything. I just cried and put my head down. Finally, after all these years, the truth was out. In my head, I was screaming, *No, I didn't tell you. Tareka told you, and you still took him back! You didn't even stand up for us. Not once.*

Granny said, "Lamika, what did he do to you all? You can trust me if you can't trust anyone else. Please tell me so I can help y'all. Clearly, you can't tell your mom anything."

Granny's face twisted with pain, but she wasn't stopping. She kept asking, demanding more details. The air was tense and my heart was hammering in my chest. The question I was too scared to even think about.

"What exactly did he do?" Granny's words hit me like a slap. "Tell me, Lamika. I need to know every single detail. Please."

My body stiffened. My hands balled into fists, but I didn't know what to do. The room spun, my mind racing as I felt trapped between the truth and the fear that telling it would destroy everything. But Granny wasn't backing down.

She wiped her tears, her voice shaking but resolute. "You have to tell me everything. I need to know, for your own safety. How did he touch you... anywhere? What did he do to you all? Did he hurt you? Tell me!"

I looked at the floor, unable to make eye contact. Every word felt like it would tear me apart. My body felt numb, but the shame and fear surged, flooding my mind like a tidal wave. I've never been asked these types of questions before.

Granny didn't stop. She crouched down, her face softening as she reached for my hand. "Please, Lamika. I have to know so I can protect you. You don't have to hide anymore. What did he do to you all?"

Her desperation felt like it was crushing me, but the truth was out there, waiting to spill. And despite my fear, despite everything I had buried inside me for so long, I knew it was time.

But Mom was standing right there, her face a mixture of anger and fear. She was also scared of what the truth would mean, but it was more than that. She didn't want us to say a word, and she didn't want anyone to know. Her silence felt like a betrayal. She was protecting him instead of us.

As Granny's questions grew louder and more urgent, I could feel Mom's eyes burning into me, willing me to stay quiet. But I couldn't. The truth was there, heavy on my chest, waiting to be spoken. Mom's face twisted in panic, but her hands shook in anger, gripping the table's edge like she might explode. She didn't want me to speak; she wanted this all to stay hidden, to remain buried under a rug.

I cleared my throat, trying to steady the tremble in my voice. I wasn't ready for this. I wasn't prepared to face the pain of remembering. But Granny was looking at me with those eyes full of hope that we could finally get some relief, that the truth would come out and we could be saved.

Mom shot me a look that made my insides move around. She wasn't angry with Granny but with me for speaking. She didn't want the world to know her business. But I couldn't go back now. I couldn't silence the truth anymore.

I took a shaky breath, the words stuck in my throat but wanting to force their way out. Slowly, I began to tell Granny what I could remember, piece by piece. It was hard, so hard, because I had spent so many years burying those memories deep down inside. At only eight years old, I didn't understand its full weight an adult would. But I understood enough to know that this was wrong, everything about it was wrong and that I couldn't keep pretending it didn't happen.

I wanted to say more, but every word felt like a piece of me was falling apart. And all the while, Mom stood there, frozen, too scared to intervene but too afraid of the truth to stop me.

The words flowed very choppy from my mouth, "He told me it better be a secret or else, that no one else would understand. He said if

I told anyone, I'd get in trouble, or worse, I'd break my family apart. I didn't know what to believe. I was scared of him but even more scared of what might happen if I told someone." I could feel the wooden edge of the chair pressing into the back of my legs, sharp and unforgiving as if to remind me there was no escape. Granny's voice was steady but carried the weight of a thousand storms, the kind that made the walls feel like they were closing in.

My sweaty fingers attempted to grip the hem of my shirt, twisting and pulling, trying to anchor myself to something solid, but the fabric was sweaty. My mouth was dry, my lips trembling as I tried to speak, but the words felt like stones lodged in my throat, unwilling to move. My words started to formulate again.

I mumbled, "He wakes us up after mom puts us to bed. He does it when no one else is around. He makes us shower with him. It is a lot to talk about." Granny fell to the floor with disappointment. I thought mom was looking at me but she was looking through me.

Echos of Hurt

I looked over to see Granny screaming and crying on the ground in front of me, and I couldn't tell if I was doing the right thing by finally speaking up or making a terrible mistake by opening my mouth. Granny's face turned pale, her eyes glistening with tears she refused to let fall. She placed a trembling hand over her mouth as if to hold back the nausea rising in her throat. Her voice broke as she whispered, "When, Lamika? When does he find the time to do all this? When?"

Her words hung in the air, sharp and accusing, but not at me at the truth I was finally spilling. I could see her body stiffen, her knuckles white as she gripped the table's edge. The pain in her voice was like a blade cutting through the room, slicing into the silence between us. My stomach churned, and I could only look at the floor, unable to answer, wishing I could erase the torment I was causing her by simply telling the truth.

I go on to mention, "He always waited until we were alone after mom had left for work, until the house was quiet, and no one could hear us if we called for help." "Even after it was over, I couldn't stop shaking. None of us gets to sleep at night or the nights to follow. Every time I closed my eyes, I could feel him there, like a shadow that wouldn't disappear. I stopped talking as much. I felt like everyone could see what happened to us like we were wearing it on our skin."

Granny, frozen in a storm of shock, darted her eyes toward Mom, who stood rooted in place, visibly torn. The weight of knowing it happened while she was gone, while she was working to provide, settled heavily on her shoulders. Neither could find words, their silence as deafening as the truth spilling into the room.

My mouth hung open, trembling as the secret I had held in for so long began to unravel. It wasn't intentional to keep it hidden; it just stayed buried, locked away where it felt safer. Now, with every word, I could feel the air dull, the room closing in on us, and the pain I had tried to bury clawing its way to the surface.

My words constantly fell out of my mouth. "He crossed lines I didn't even know existed. It felt wrong, but I didn't know how to stop it. I just wanted it to be over. I wanted to disappear." The thought in my mind started flowing, "I was too young to fight back, too scared to say no. The tears filled my puffy eyes. I said, "I kept thinking maybe if I stayed quiet, he would stop. But he didn't, and I couldn't do anything to make him."

With Mom being with him, I figured he loved us like his own children. In the beginning, he seemed to care; his actions mimicked what I thought love should look like. He played the role so well, his smiles warm and his words gentle that I believed it. But the betrayal was sharp, like a knife I never saw coming. What he portrayed was a mask, and the truth behind it shattered everything I thought I knew about trust and family.

I explained to mom and granny, "I used to think he cared about us. He was always nice when other people were around, giving us gifts and spending time with us. But when we were alone, it was like he was someone else entirely. I didn't know which person was real." I couldn't stop talking about it because this was the first time I had their attention.

I was daydreaming with my watery eyes facing the ceiling. Looking back now, I wish I had spoken up sooner. I wish someone had noticed the signs or asked the right questions. I wish I hadn't been so scared to tell the truth. I didn't know how to ask for help. I didn't even know I was allowed to. The consequences lingered if he found out I told him as well.

Granny was screaming so loud that she didn't hear most of what my small, trembling voice was trying to say. Her eyes burned with disgust as she stared at Mom, who stood frozen with guilt and shame. Across from me, my sister sat silently, tears streaming down her face. She looked numb, a sharp contrast to the sister I knew, the one who usually spoke up for us both. But today, she didn't say a single word, leaving me to explain everything to Granny. My sister looked at me in fear, like *what did you do?* She knew if we told anyone what he threatened us with. I could feel the heaviness in my chest, but deep down, I believed someone had to know.

Someone needed to hear the truth, someone who could help us, someone who could finally end this nightmare. With all her love and anger, Granny did everything she could to help us. But after everything came to light, Mom still took us home. Unsettling for us because I let the cat out the bag and if he finds out... he will kill us.

Days passed in uneasy silence, and nothing felt normal. Then, one afternoon, Granny showed up, her voice calm but firm. "I'm taking the kids," she said, her eyes locked on Mom, daring her to object. Mom didn't stop her; whether out of exhaustion or fear, we didn't know.

Granny's determination didn't stop there. She called the police, contacted Grandpa Villie, Mom's biological father, and pushed for answers and help from the family. Granny told anyone who would listen so word got out quickly. When Mom found out about the report, everything began to unravel. Fear and guilt consumed her, and she panicked.

Then came the call that changed everything. "Hello, is this Dina?" a voice asked. "Yes," Mom answered, her voice trembling. "You need to bring the kids in for evaluation." Mom did not know that was granny's intention when she picked us up.

We didn't fully understand what was happening as Granny drove us to the hospital. Inside, the hospital was cold and quiet, the smell of antiseptic filling the air. Nurses led us into a small room where doctors asked questions we didn't know how to answer. The examinations were invasive, and the silence in the room was deafening. When the results came back, they confirmed the truth we were too afraid to say out loud: we had been violated.

Granny didn't cry; her heartbreak simmered beneath a quiet fury. Once mom found out, she spiraled, torn between guilt and denial. Meanwhile, we bounced between Granny's determination to protect us and Mom's desperate grasp to keep us close.

But going back to Granny's house wasn't simple. Mom wanted us home. She still thought she could fix everything, but she didn't know how or maybe she didn't want to. We felt torn between the safety Granny tried to give us and the loyalty we felt to Mom.

We bounced between their houses for a while, the tension following us wherever we went. No place felt like home, and no one had the answers we needed. But one thing was certain: the truth was out, and nothing would ever be the same again.

Before we could settle, Grandpa Villie began showing up whether we were home or at grannies, his face etched with concern. He pressed Granny for answers she wasn't ready to give. He knew too much about the chaos, the late-night card games, the neglect. Everything was spiraling out of control, but one thing was clear: the truth couldn't be buried any longer.

Over at grannies house we were secluded to the back room. We could not use the bathroom or eat until they got up. We had to hold our bowels for long lengthy hours until they realized we were there. We would cry ourselves to sleep in pain at night. They hid us away from the world in that back room. They did not want anyone to know we were there. One night, they had another late night card game with drinking, smoking, and laughs. A woman stumbled into the back room door because she thought it was the bathroom. She said, "Oh, I'm sorry for going in the wrong door. WAIT, aint y'all Dina's children?" We shook our heads yes in despair. Grandpa Majesty came to the back yelling, "Did they come out of that room bothering you? I'm going to tear them a new one." She said, "No, I went in the wrong door." She shut the door and said "Dina has some nice looking children, they are so precious." Grandpa Majesty with his mysterious laugh chuckled it off.

We got whoopens mainly from him everyday we stayed there. It was his mission to beat us and go back to bed. We were forgotten about most of the time. We had to knock on the inside of the door to get their attention if we heard footsteps. We were ordered to never open the door. We had to wait for them to open the door. We used to get excited to hear them walking around and awake. We used to sneak into the bathroom if we couldn't hold it any longer. If grandpa was already up watching shows once he dozed off was the best time. Granny slept through everything. The normal time they woke up was late in the evening, the sun would be going down. They would feed us, tell us to use the bathroom, and back into the room we would go. We rarely bathed at their house. It was far, few, and in between.

Granny, exhausted and desperate, called Villie one night. "I need help with these kids," she pleaded. "This can't keep going like this." From one house to another, one extreme to the next, we were like pinballs in a survival game. No stability. No peace. Just endless bouncing, each landing more chaotic than the last. Grandpa Villie knew kids should not be in a party house all day every day. He was receiving phone calls all the time from the school due to us not attending.

Beneath the Surface

Granny took us to Walmart, and as we walked through the store, my eyes always went straight to the missing kids' pictures, saying, *Have You Seen Me?* In the 1990s, the grocery store had a bulletin board near the entrance filled with photos of missing children, their innocent faces staring back at shoppers as a haunting reminder of those still lost. I also noticed that in school, around lunchtime, they would print their faces on the backs of milk cartons. They were desperate pleas for help in the form of innocent smiles frozen in time. I couldn't help but wonder, *What if I was one of those kids?* Did they have a better life, as much as we were suffering?

I would look at the faces on the milk cartons and wonder if they were happier than me when the photo was taken. Maybe they were safe now, far away from the things that hurt them. Maybe they had a family that loved them or a home where they felt safe and didn't have to worry all the time. Sometimes, I wished I could be like them someone who could disappear and not be stuck in the havoc I was in. Maybe they found a way out, which was better than staying where I was.

There were days when I felt so alone like I didn't belong anywhere, and I'd wonder if they thought the same way before they were missing. Sometimes, the weight of everything felt so heavy that I thought maybe it would be easier if I just wasn't here anymore, if I could just disappear like those kids on the milk cartons. But then I'd remember there was still hope for us. I still had a chance to find a way out, to get away from the pain. So I held onto that because deep down, I knew I had to keep going, even when it felt like it was too much. I had to continue to fight for life when it came to my siblings.

Maybe life would be better, maybe the things we'd gone through, the pain, confusion, and fear could all be erased. I longed for a different life, one free from the dysfunction we were trapped in, but no matter how hard I wished, it didn't change our reality. The feeling of wanting to escape was suffocating and overwhelming, and yet there was no way out.

I began to realize that even in the hardest moments, there were small pieces of light guiding me forward. I started noticing the little things that made life feel softer: the sound of laughter, the warmth of sunlight through a window, the comfort of knowing I could still hope. I learned that love didn't always have to come from others; it could start within me. Every time I chose to smile, to keep going, or to believe things could get better, I was slowly rebuilding myself. I wasn't invisible. I was still here, still growing, still becoming someone stronger than the pain that tried to break me.

But, despite it all, life didn't unfold that way. Deep down, I always had faith that Mom would find her way back to the amazing person she once was. I knew in my heart that God would make a way out of no way. We wanted to stay with Mom through thick and thin. We were all in this together, and no matter the storms we faced, we held on to each other, hoping for a brighter tomorrow.

We were back at mom's house and someone knocked on the door. I peeked through the blinds, and I saw Grandpa Villie standing there, looking like he was carrying the weight of the world on his shoulders. I froze for a second, unsure if I should wake Mom or just let him in. I tried shaking her awake, but she didn't stir. Grandpa's voice came through the door, low and urgent. "Lamika, let me in."

I didn't think twice. I slid the door open and let him in. We were so happy to see him. He didn't look like he came to visit, though. He looked worried and confused.

The moment he stepped inside, the air seemed to sit still. Grandpa's eyes scanned the room, and he saw the emptiness that had become our life. The house was cold and barren, the refrigerator and cabinets practically bare. He checked the shelves, and there was nothing but wood chips and crumbs. I knew then he could smell the neglect, the absence of care. We hadn't bathed in days, maybe weeks. And I could see it in his face that he was hurting for us.

His gaze fell on our small bodies huddled together on the floor. He saw us sitting on the floor sharing a half-open can, and his eyes welled up. Tears blurred his vision, and I could see his jaw tighten with the effort of holding it all in. To walk into a place like this, to see his grandkids struggling in the most basic ways, was more than anyone could bear.

"I'm about to take y'all away from y'all mom," he said, his voice shaky in despair. There was no hesitation. He didn't care about the hows or the whys; he just knew we couldn't survive much longer in that place. He genuinely felt deep down that we wouldn't survive a few more weeks in that state of surrounds. Our bodies, frail and withered away from the lack of nourishment, told the silent story of our prolonged hunger. And he wasn't going to let us be lost in it anymore.

He stormed past us toward her room, his shoes thudding against the floor. He kicked open Mom's bedroom door to see her lying on a mattress on the floor. The scene he found there was nothing short of a nightmare. There she was, tangled in the sheets with some man, both of them still knocked out cold. Grandpa's voice broke the silence. "Get up!" he bellowed, his words snapping through the air like thunder. "Get the hell out of here!" Grandpa's voice, so deep and powerful, making your insides vibrate with its intensity.

The man, terrified out of his sleep, scrambled to his feet, wide-eyed and disoriented. He ran out the door with his shoes in hand. Grandpa wasn't having it. "DINA, GET UP! I'm calling the police if you don't move now!" He glared at her, his fists clenched, "What did you do with the money I gave you for the kids? Why don't you have any food here? You're sleeping all day with kids at home? What the hell is going on?"

Mom sat up, rubbing her eyes, her voice groggy. "Dad, what are you doing here?" She quickly threw on some clothes, trying to tidy up the mess around her, but Grandpa wasn't here for that. He didn't want another excuse either. He wanted to know why there was no food in the house.

"I'm taking these kids from you," he said, his voice as firm as iron. "You need to get yourself together."

He turned to us, and without a second thought, he said, "Go get in the car. NOW." His voice is deep and sharp.

We didn't think twice from the way his voice echoed through the house. We just did what he said. And for the first time in a long time, I felt like maybe, just maybe, things could get better. Grandpa was taking us away from all of this. From the turmoil. From the fear. From the uncertainty. He was our way out.

Mind Drifting Fear

We could hear the yelling from inside the house all the way to the car. The raw emotion in Grandpa's voice echoed through the tension, and I could feel the pain he carried. To see his daughter in such a state that her lifestyle has taken on and to see us his grandchildren suffering because of it was more than anyone should have to fathom.

As I sat in the car with my siblings, I could only stare back at the house. The thought of being away from my mom, the woman who had brought us into this world, the happy times, and also many of our struggles felt impossible. It was the hardest thing I had ever faced. The pain of separation was breathtaking and unbearable.

We had been with her through so much. Through the highs and the lows. Through the joy and the heartbreak. We had seen her at her best, and we had seen her at her worst. No matter what, we had always stood by her side. We had promised, without words, that we would go all the way with her. So why did it feel so wrong to leave?

Then, the tears started. We all cried. The car was filled with the sound of our sobs, the tears falling down our faces like waterfalls, drenching our little shirts. Our noses ran, and we sounded like howling dogs, each of us screaming and crying, wishing we could just run back to her.

This was one of the saddest moments of my life. My mind raced, spinning like a whirlwind. I needed answers, and I needed them now.

- How would she survive without us?
- Would this make things worse for her?
- Would it make her stronger, like Grandpa hoped, so that we could come home one day?
- Would she even notice that we were gone?
- Would she be okay without us?

It may sound crazy, but at that moment, I would have rather stayed with her than started over somewhere else. I was only 8 years old, but I could only think about her. She was our mother. And even though it hurt more than words could say, I still loved her dearly.

Grandpa comes fuming out of the house, slamming the door behind him with a thunderous BOOM that makes us flinch in the car. As we were bunched up against the window, looking. His heavy footsteps echo as he stomps to the car, his face tight with fury and something deeper pain. Without hesitation, he throws himself into the driver's seat, yanking the door shut with a loud thud.

Mom comes running out, her voice cracking as she screams, "Don't take my kids away from me, Dad!" Her desperate cries pierce through the air, but Grandpa doesn't flinch. He locks the doors in one swift motion, the metallic click sealing us inside as Mom grabs the passenger door handle, pulling and shaking it violently. The latch retracts uselessly, snapping back to the car.

Inside, we're panicked, tears streaming down our faces as we cry out for her. Our small hands pressed against the car windows, smearing them as we tried to reach for her. "Mom! Mom!" we wail, our voices breaking under the weight of fear and helplessness.

She yells through the glass, her voice full of desperation and a promise, "I'll come for y'all! I'll be there to get you, I swear!"

Grandpa slams his foot on the gas, the tires screeching as the car lurches forward. Mom stumbles back, narrowly avoiding the rear tires. We twist in our seats to look back at her, wanting one last glimpse, but Grandpa roars, "Don't turn around! Y'all hear me? Face forward!"

We sit frozen, sobbing uncontrollably as he continues, his voice sharp and heavy with authority. "Y'all be quiet with all that whining! This is what's best for y'all until your mom gets herself together."

His voice cracks for the first time as he continues, softer now, "She can't even take care of herself, let alone three children. These drugs... they've got a hold on her."

The car begins to slow as Grandpa's grip on the wheel loosens slightly. His shoulders slump, and his deep, trembling voice carries the weight of years living with regret. "I should've been around more. I should've done better by her... Maybe if I stayed with Sharlean, none of this would've happened." he sobbed silently.

The car falls quiet except for the sound of our sniffles and his heavy breathing. The tears rolling down his weathered face catch the sunlight, a rare and heartbreaking vulnerability showing through his stern demeanor. At that moment, I could feel something eating him up on the inside, a battle between the guilt of what he thought he failed to do as a father and the necessity of stepping in as a grandfather.

I realized then how much it must have broken him to take us away. It wasn't just anger that fueled his decision, it was the deep, unrelenting pain of seeing his daughter lose herself and knowing her children were caught in the wreckage. Word got around fast from granny telling everyone or situation.

Even as a child, I sensed that he carried an unbearable weight. He was doing what he knew was right, but the question floated in the air like a haunting ghost: *If we stayed with Mom, where would we be?* We weren't turning around that day and while a part of us never stopped looking back, I understood the terrifying, confusing truth: Grandpa wasn't saving us from our mother; he was saving us for her, giving her the space and the shock needed to find her way back, while taking the responsibility for our safety onto his own trembling shoulders.

The screech of the tires faded, replaced by the relentless, quiet hum of the road beneath us. The better life was waiting, yes, but its foundation was built on a moment of irreversible, necessary violence. As the lights of our old town disappeared behind us, I closed my eyes. We were moving forward, and though every mile was a heavy, complicated step away from the life we knew, our lives were now a promise, a burden, and a desperate act of love carried by a heartbroken man. We were safe now, and that safety, built from such profound loss, felt like the first difficult breath of a brand new life.

Epilogue

Looking back now, I can see the threads of my journey weaving together in ways I could never have imagined. There were moments of pain, joy, and uncertainty, but each one led me to where I am today. The road wasn't always easy, and the challenges I faced often seemed insurmountable. But in every struggle, there was growth. In every setback, there was a lesson.

I've learned that life doesn't always go according to plan. Sometimes, we find ourselves lost, wandering down paths we didn't choose. But what matters is how we rise after the fall and rebuild after the cracks because it's in those broken places where our true strength is forged.

This chapter is a testament to the power of resilience, of never giving up even when the odds seem stacked against us. Through it all, I've discovered a truth I wish I had known all along: I am enough. I always was.

Acknowledgments

This journey would not have been possible without the unwavering support and love of so many incredible people.

First and foremost, I want to thank GOD!

I want to thank my mom, whose strength, wisdom, and love laid the foundation for everything I am today. Her courage to find her own way back allowed us to forge a relationship built on forgiveness and enduring love.

To my brother and sister, thank you for always being by my side. Our shared journey did not break us; it fused us into an unbreakable team. Your laughter, your support, and our love for one another are the greatest triumphs of our story.

To the people who fed us, thank you for giving more than just food; you gave comfort, kindness, and hope when we needed it most.

A special thank you to my grandpa, Villie, whose wisdom continues to guide me, even in his absence. His decision to rescue us was an act of profound love that forever changed our trajectory.

To Cynthia, for your unwavering love for us it meant the world.

To granny, for stepping in the best way she knew how. You are appreciated and loved.

To my husband, who has believed in me through every challenge and doubt, thank you for being my rock. Your love and encouragement pushed me to keep going.

To my children, who have given me a reason to keep pushing forward, you are my purpose, light, and motivation.

To my cousin Cyn and Shecosha, thank you for your unwavering belief in me.

Finally, thank you to the readers for reading my story. I hope it inspires you to embrace your own potential, knowing that the greatest strength always comes from within.

With all my love and gratitude, Tamika

About The Author

Tamika is a dedicated Registered Nurse with nearly two decades of experience, a passionate entrepreneur, and a storyteller with a mission. Hailing from Indiana, Tamika draws upon a life full of challenges, triumphs, and transformations to inspire others through their writing. As the author of the *Moore to Lyfe* series, she aims to share their journey in raw, relatable, and empowering ways, helping readers find strength and meaning in their own lives.

Balancing a thriving career and a multitude of business ventures, Tamika is committed to creating opportunities for others to grow, heal, and succeed. When not writing or working, Tamika enjoys reflecting on life's lessons, cherishing meaningful memories, and building a legacy of strength, hope, and purpose.

www.ingramcontent.com/pod-product-compliance
Lightning Source LLC
LaVergne TN
LVHW021952060526
838201LV00049B/1682